T0265259

A How-To Guide for Business School Practitioners

A How-To Guide for Business School Practitioners

By

Moira Tolan
Mount Saint Mary College

Tracey Niemotko
Marist College

INFORMATION AGE PUBLISHING, INC.
Charlotte, NC • www.infoagepub.com

Library of Congress Cataloging-in-Publication Data

CIP record for this book is available from the Library of Congress
http://www.loc.gov

ISBNs: 979-8-88730-656-8 (Paperback)

979-8-88730-657-5 (Hardcover)

979-8-88730-658-2 (ebook)

CONTENTS

CHAPTER 1

THE DIMINISHING VALUE OF A BUSINESS DEGREE

ABSTRACT

Business programs at American colleges and universities thrived for many years, despite a general reluctance to promote the capitalist ideals that underscore American business achievement. Many of these schools also failed to apply to themselves some of the business models that they are assumed to be teaching. For the past several years, however, many small and under-endowed institutions have been forced to face their financial problems through closure, mergers, or other forms of restructuring.

Keywords: business schools, declining enrollment, capitalism, differentiation

INTRODUCTION

In this chapter, we discuss the frequent, ironic failure of colleges and business programs to recognize profit as a motive for operating effectively. Over the past 30 years, many administrators in higher education have become dependent on an ever-increasing influx of federal student loan money and endowments that were growing rapidly in an expanding stock market (Bennett & Wilezol, 2012). Chung and Brown (2021) recently reported in the *The Wall Street Journal* that in 2021 many large endowment portfolios were boosted by the soaring stock market and investments in venture capital. For example, "the University of Minnesota's endowment gained 49.2% for the year ending June 30, 2021, while Brown University's endowment notched a return of more than 50%, said people familiar with their returns, which aren't yet public" (para. 2). Given this steady stream

A How-To Guide for Business School Practitioners, pp. 1–12
Copyright © 2024 by Information Age Publishing
www.infoagepub.com

of funds, college administrators frequently neglect results-oriented performance. This indifference has played a detrimental role in preventing the continual improvement and growth that business programs need to remain viable.

Many business programs have failed to respond to the changing demands of consumers, including prospective students, their parents, and employers. Such programs, whose very mission is to teach students how to generate capital in a principled fashion, be responsive to customers, and generate value, have, incongruously, come up short in all three areas. Consequently, employers, students, parents, and others question the value of a college degree in general and the study of business in particular. Disenchanted with the cost and value of many college programs, these dissatisfied "customers" often point to the remarkable success in business of America's best-known billionaire college drop-outs—Bill Gates, founder of Microsoft, Steven Jobs, founder of Apple, Mark Zuckerberg, founder of Facebook, and others. The pandemic of 2020 and the interruptions that it caused in the delivery of college programs served to illuminate some of the problems with colleges and universities to prospective students and their families. It allowed many to reflect on whether what they were getting in the "physical classroom" before the pandemic was relevant and worth the significant expense that it demands.

Paradoxically, business school administrators are often dismissive of the concept of profit, the balance of revenues that an enterprise retains after expenses are paid. Some key practitioners educating business students today frequently deride principled capitalism itself. In a kind of fun-house mirror reversal, they denigrate making a profit—even when that profit is made legitimately, fairly, ethically, and benefits society at large. A recent article by Admati (2019), a prominent Stanford business school professor, summarizes the feelings of many academics in that he renounces a capitalist system in which ethical breaches can cause great dysfunction, and supports, as many academics do, additional government intervention to rein in free markets.

Many academic insiders fault their business schools for teaching market capitalism techniques that led to ethical crises and an overall mistrust of the capitalist system. Admati (2019) writes, "Whereas having ethical and caring corporate leaders is obviously helpful, governments are what embody our collective action. They often have the most appropriate tools to promote social well-being and prevent social harm." This type of thinking is counterintuitive to the principled capitalism that was espoused by many of the foremost proponents of the system, including Adam Smith, Frederick von Hayek, Ludwig von Mises, and Milton Friedman. These economists recognized the self-correcting features in the system and its great potential for raising societal standards of living while providing a mechanism to expose corruption.

As a result of the indifference to basic capitalist tools, estimates of income, expenses, and profit margins are often constructed haphazardly by academics, and budgets in many business programs are not strictly followed. In the private sector or for-profit world, such behavior would spell disaster, and failure to generate a profit would rapidly lead to bankruptcy. In higher education, however, ever-increasing numbers of students, federal subsidies, existing endowments, and new donors can insulate those making poor business decisions from their organic consequences. Readily funded student loans have also increased administrators' and faculty members' budgetary complacency and encouraged them to neglect profit maximization. Government intervention in the form of subsidies to students and academic institutions during the pandemic will most likely have a further detrimental effect on the performance of academic institutions. Proposed student loan forgiveness programs will also send signals to the market that will further erode individual accountability towards making appropriate educational choices.

Over the past two decades, tuition costs at colleges and universities have increased at a much higher rate than other commodities that are measured by the Consumer Price Index. For example, at a time when the total consumer price index inflation increased by approximately 50% (from August 2000 to August 2020), the average tuition and fees at private national universities have jumped 144%, out-of-state tuition and fees at public national universities have risen 165%, and in-state tuition and fees at public national universities have grown the most, increasing 212% (Boyington & Kerr, 2020). Despite these extreme price increases, colleges and universities have been buoyed by ever-growing funds regardless of whether they have balanced their budgets, ended each year in the black, or accrued large debts. Vast waves of federally subsidized loan money have provided supplemental protection for college administrators, faculty, and staff and encouraged relaxing vigilance in all areas of business operations. In addition, endowments that generate significant returns provide a cushion to institutions, which may shield them from being compelled to operate efficiently.

College administrators continually exhibit complacency towards their internal operations, and, increasingly, their business programs fail to prepare students to work successfully in a free-market economy that seeks workers who can practice what principled capitalism requires. Gary Hamel (2012), a management theorist who the WSJ has deemed the world's most influential business thinker, has proposed a "reimagining" of the way that we think about "principled capitalism." He notes that the need for a principled capitalism "is more urgent than ever, not just as an effort to escape reform and regulation from the outside, but to restore the public trust, to repair the moral fabric of the system, and to unleash the innovation required to tackle the world's most pressing and important challenges." The questions that Hamel asks businesses to address, and which are attached in Appendix A, are those that have always been considered being relevant to participation in a free market. We argue that Hamel's principled capitalism is the same as the early, free-market, capitalist writers and advocates proposed.

Steve Forbes (2009), similarly, in extolling the virtues of a capitalist society, writes, "It is unfortunate that capitalism has been denigrated by uninformed people for many years, and that the criticism rears its ugly head during economic crises. We keep hearing from people from other countries that move to the United States that this country is the best country in the world, and the primary reason is capitalism: allowing people to live the American Dream." As economist Milton Friedman (1962) clearly pointed out when promoting the benefits of capitalism, he could not find an example of any society in which economic freedom and personal and political freedom did not coexist.

Business school should be regarded as playing a critical role in the dissemination of principled capitalist ideals. However, the business curricula at most schools have been stagnant and often fail to inspire students toward principled capitalism. Principled capitalism is often not taught explicitly at all, and as mentioned earlier, business itself and the profit motive are often demeaned. Business schools often fail to connect capitalism to societal benefits in a meaningful way, as Hamel suggests in the questions he poses to companies.

Colleges and universities that fail to operate with a business mindset set the "tone from the top" that often translates into teaching from a non-business perspective—which, in turn, may undermine students' understanding of how principled capitalism should operate. Thus, students' ability to understand business may also be challenged, perhaps making them apologetic about studying business, and diminishing their abilities to be happy, productive, successful employees whose work will benefit themselves and others. Moreover, this kind of academic preparation will not shape students to be firm believers in and supporters of a principled free enterprise system or equip them to accurately critique other less ethical and democratic, as well as poorly managed economic systems.

Dramatic technical innovations and societal changes, highlighted by the recent pandemic, have also disrupted the effectiveness of many traditional business programs. This book outlines several strategies that business program administrators and faculty might adopt to triumph over the turbulent forces that continue to batter their programs and render them financially unstable.

The Fall From Grace

During our many years working in academia, we have frequently witnessed a lack of commitment on the part of colleges and business programs, in particular, to address financial realities by creating value for their "customers." There is often an ongoing tension at institutions of higher learning between those who propose changes to academic programs or operating systems and those who cling to traditional ways of functioning. Faculty members are repeatedly reminded through convocations, investitures, commencements, capping ceremonies, and the like that colleges and universities descended from a long line of influential educating entities, going back to Ancient Greece and Rome.

Academia's deep-seated traditions have frequently resulted in static systems and cultures that resist change. However, these systems and change-resistant cultures have become a luxury that most colleges and universities can no longer afford. Many of them are staggering under substantial financial burdens, generating financial insecurities that put their very survival at risk. As Chandler (2010) writes in discussing his study regarding the resistance to change in higher education institutions (HEIs):

> HEIs are found to have particular cultures different to many organisations in the private sector and resistance to change in HEIs appears to stem from a number of sources, some of which are related to organizational culture, including: the faculty members, a sense of territory, time issues, resource issues, a strong sense of tradition, leadership, communication, unions and individual autonomy.

Exacerbating general financial and budgetary issues, many colleges and universities face a declining population of high school graduates. The number of high school graduates has decreased in most of the country and most likely will not increase again until 2024 (Lapovsky, 2018). In 2014, all six New England states were projected to suffer double-digit decline rates compared to 2008 (Warren Interstate Commission for Higher Education, 2014). In addition, international student enrollment has been dropping in recent years (Redden, 2019). Of concern to business educators should be that during the 2018–2019 academic year, math/computer science surpassed business/management as the second-most-popular field for international students. The number of students studying math and computer science increased by 9.4%, while the number studying business fell by 7.1% (Redden, 2019). These numbers were similar in 2022 when 21% studied math and computer science, 19.8% studied engineering and 15.5% studied business (Open Doors, 2023).

Moreover, the international pandemic of 2020 has heightened this decline, with 88% of institutions surveyed expecting international student enrollment to decline in the 2020–2021 school year and 30% expecting a "substantial" decline (Smith-Barrow, 2020). These trends are alarming, and the competition among business programs for traditional students has understandably become fierce. Unfortunately, plans to counter this grim demographic forecast were not addressed at many institutions until the admissions crisis struck.

The President of Cardinal Stritch University in Milwaukee, Wisconsin recently announced the closing of the 85-year-old Roman Catholic institution and cited "fiscal realities, downward enrollment trends, the [coronavirus] pandemic, the need for more resources and the mounting operational and facility challenges" (Moody, 2023). Similarly, in recent months, religiously affiliated colleges including Iowa Wesleyan University, Presentation College, Finlandia University, Holy Names University and Living Arts College have announced their plans to close while others, like Medaille University, have been absorbed into financially viable institutions (Moody, 2023). Twenty-seven percent of college presidents surveyed by *Inside Higher Ed* said in 2023 that their college should consider a merger within the next five years. Surprisingly, amid all of these grim financial reckonings, 8 in 10 presidents who responded indicated that they believed their college would be financially stable over the next decade (Moody, 2023). This type of thinking, without proper consideration of financial realities and changing market conditions, may further stifle possible strategic ventures that could help colleges and universities avert disasters such as those we are currently witnessing.

The financial and operational challenges that colleges and universities currently face differ from their experiences over the last few decades. For many years, student loans gave middle-class American families the illusion that they could afford extremely high-priced academic experiences. As huge debt burdens are publicized, and students holding the debt are increasingly underemployed after graduation, families are seeking alternatives to the traditional college experience. Some options include completing an associate degree instead of pursuing a higher-priced bachelor's degree.

Moody (2020) reports that a recent Georgetown study has determined that 27% of workers with an associate degree earn more than the median for workers with a bachelor's degree. Coding boot camps also provide high average starting salaries for their graduates, as do apprenticeships. Additionally, more students are pursuing online education or the military to defray future education costs (Moody, 2020). Moreover, there is a growing trend of large, innovative corporations hiring and training workers who do not possess a bachelor's degree. These companies, including IBM, Google, and Apple, to name a few, have committed to in-house training for employees to develop skillsets that will be of strategic benefit.

Ironically, as the public becomes more and more concerned with student debt and less convinced of the long-term value of a college education, most colleges and universities have continued to address their own financial shortfalls by raising tuition, board, and room rates. In the past, these costs were met by student borrowing, which the U.S. government readily supported. According to Martin (2017):

> Students at public four-year institutions paid an average of $3,190 in tuition for the 1987–1988 school year, with prices adjusted to reflect 2017 dollars. Thirty years later, that average has risen to $9,970 for the 2017–2018 school year. That's a 213 percent increase.

This is in stark contrast to the consumer purchasing power in that:

> Today's real average wage (that is, the wage after accounting for inflation) has about the same purchasing power it did 40 years ago. And what wage gains there have been have mostly flowed to the highest-paid tier of workers. (Desilver, 2018)

The difference between tuition costs 20 years ago and those costs today at private schools is also stark. "In 1988, the average tuition in the United States for a private nonprofit four-year institution was $15,160 in 2017 dollars. For the 2017–2018 school year, it's $34,740, a 129 percent increase" (Martin, 2017). These increases are met with scrutiny by a large number of consumers. Families are often dismayed when they have taken on debt that cannot be justified by employment options for their college graduates in a changing economy. A simple business risk-benefit analysis shows that this kind of "bet" is unlikely to be profitable. "Student debt impacts borrowers over time by raising debt burdens, lowering credit scores and ultimately, limiting the purchasing power of those with student debt. Because young people are disproportionately burdened by student debt, they will be less able to participate in—and help grow—the economy in the long run" (Hess, 2021).

Despite societal changes and significant tuition increases, most colleges and universities have done little to differentiate themselves. Basic economic principles display that these increases are untenable. Many academic institutions now face a target market that can afford to be selective. As mentioned above, families of college-age students are exploring other options instead of a four-year baccalaureate degree. Moreover, the global pandemic has highlighted alternatives to the standard classroom/dormitory model.

College administrators may profess to promote their institutions' mission even if it comes at the price of sacrificing potential profit. However, even during the years of sharp price increases, many colleges have not stayed true to their missions. For example, a vast majority of "religious" colleges and universities have either totally turned away from their original missions or have significantly watered them down. The same is true for schools whose mission was to provide students with immersion in the liberal arts or to develop students into well-rounded individuals. There is a dearth of research that looks into the impact of mission erosion on financial viability, but it appears that this trend has diminished differentiating factors of religiously affiliated institutions.

The movement away from purported missions has created marketing issues that have never been fully addressed. Bishirjian (2019) writes:

> Today, there are only a handful of religious colleges and universities that stand fast against the cultural decline and moral laxity that shapes American society. For that reason, in early March of last year, when I was invited to give a presentation about higher education to an organization of Catholic citizens in Chicago, I chose as my topic the decline of religious colleges. And since I was speaking to a Catholic audience, I focused on the decline of such Catholic colleges as the University of Notre Dame, Georgetown University, Loyola Marymount, Gonzaga, and Marquette. The commitment of all five to the magisterium of the Church has declined to the extent that concerned alumni have organized groups opposed to further decline.

As in all marketing, if there is a disjoint between what a company claims to produce or stand for and what they are actually providing, consumers get confused and begin to look elsewhere for comparable products and services.

In addition to student loans and mission fulfillment concerns, large endowments worked to feed the illusion of organizational success, making value creation for students a non-priority. In 2021, college and university endowments posted their most robust annual outcomes in 35 years, according to data from the Wilshire Trust Universe Comparison Service and reported by Bloomberg. The median return before fees was 27% in the 2021 fiscal year. By comparison, the college and university endowments had a median return of 2.6% in 2020 and a median return of 6% in 2019. In addition, endowments of at least $500 million (about 200) reported extraordinary median returns of 34% in 2021. In the 12 months between June 2021 and June, 2022, the return to the endowments was starkly different that in the previous years, losing a median 10.2% before fees. The funds with assets over 500 million, however, outperformed substantially better with a gain of .9% (Bloomberg.com). These numbers are cause for alarm, especially at the small and medium-sized institutions that counted on the continued growth of these funds as a buffer from other market pressures.

Although these returns add an additional layer of wealth to the endowments of colleges and universities with significant holdings, they may also widen the wealth gap among higher education institutions. For instance, many colleges that lack endowments or are marginally invested may not benefit financially from market returns in the same way (Whitford, 2021). Rather than accumulating wealth, some colleges tap into their endowments to pay operating expenses and balance their operating budgets.

In Chapter 2, we consider in further detail some of the challenges currently facing many of the nation's colleges and universities, such as the dissemination of a "college for all" philosophy, the student loan crisis, a proliferation of expensive amenities, potentially irrelevant academic programs, and the prevalence of an anti-capitalist bias that runs counter to long-term competitive success. Chapter 3 offers some macro solutions for college administrators to consider and possibly adopt.

REFERENCES

Admati, A. (2019, September 2). How business schools can help restore trust in capitalism. *Harvard Business Review*. https://hbr.org/2019/09/how-business-schools-can-help-restore-trust-in-capitalism

Bennett, W., & Wilezol, D. (2013). *Is college worth it?* Thomas Nelson.

Bishirjian, R. (2019, June 21). The decline of religious colleges and universities. *The Imaginative Conservative*. https://theimaginativeconservative.org/2019/06/decline-religious-colleges-universities-richard-bishirjian.html

Boyington, B., & Kerr, E. (2020). 20 years of tuition growth at national universities. *U.S. News*. https://www.usnews.com/education/bestcolleges/paying-for-college/articles/2017-09-20/see-20-years-of-tuition-growth-atnational-universities

Chandler, N. (2010). *Braced for turbulence: Understanding and managing resistance to change in the higher education sector.* Budapest Business School. https://www.researchgate.net/publication/258256802_Braced_for_Turbulence_Understanding_and_Managing_Resistance_to_Change_in_the_Higher_Education_Sector

Chung, J., & Brown, E., (2021, September 21). University endowments mint billions in golden era of venture capital. *The Wall Street Journal*. https://www.wsj.com/articles/university-endowments-mint-billions-in-golden-era-of-venture-capital-11632907802

Desilver, D. (2018, August 7). *For most U.S.workers, real wages have barely budged in decades*. Pew Research Center. https://www.pewresearch.org/short-reads/2018/08/07/for-most-us-workers-real-wages-have-barely-budged-for-decades/#:~:text=In%20fact%2C%20despite%20some%20ups,highest%2Dpaid%20tier%20of%20workers

Forbes, S. (2009). *How capitalism will save us*. Crown Publishing Group.

Friedman, M. (1962). *Capitalism and freedom*. University of Chicago Press.

Hamel, G. (2012, March 20). *Reimagining capitalism—as principled, patient, and truly social. Opensource. Com*. https://opensource.com/business/12/3/reimagining-capitalism%E2%80%94-principled-patient-and-truly-social

Hess, A. J. (2021, July 2). *3 ways student debt impacts the economy.* CNBC. https://www.cnbc.com/2021/07/02/3-ways-student-debt-impacts-the-economy.html#:~:text=Student%20debt%20impacts%20borrowers%20over,economy%20in%20the%20long%20run

Lapovsky, L. (2018, February 6). The changing business model for colleges and universities. *Forbes.* https://www.forbes.com/sites/lucielapovsky/2018/02/06/the-changing-business-model-for-colleges-and-universities/?sh=63171f005ed5

Martin, E. (2017). *Here's how much more expensive it is for you to go to college than it was for your parents.* CNBC.com. https://www.cnbc.com/2017/11/29/how-much-college-tuition-has-increased-from-1988-to-2018.html

Moody, J. (2023, April 12). *Cardinal Stritch to close.* Inside Higher Ed https://www.insidehighered.com/news/quick-takes/2023/04/1---1/cardinal-stritch-u-close-endsemester#:~:text=Cardinal%20Stritch%20University%2C%20in%20Milwaukee,different%20path%20we%20could%20pursue.

Moody, J. (2020, October 28). Alternatives to a 4-year college: What to know. *U.S. News and World Report.* https://www.usnews.com/education/best-colleges/articles/alternatives-to-a-4-year-college-what-to-know

Open Doors Data.org. (2023). https://opendoorsdata.org/fast_facts/fast-facts-2022/

Redden, E. (2019). *Number of enrolled international students drops.* Inside Higher Ed. https://www.insidehighered.com/admissions/article/2019/11/18/international-enrollments-declined-undergraduate-graduate-and

Smith-Barrow, D. (2020, May 22). Losing international students because of the pandemic will damage colleges financially. *The Hechinger Report.* https://hechingerreport.org/losing-international-students-because-of-the-pandemic-will-damage-colleges-financially/

Whitford, E. (2021, August 4). *Endowments post highest returns since 1986.* Inside Higher Ed. https://www.insidehighered.com/news/2021/08/04/endowments-post-strong-returns-fiscal-2021-early-data-show

APPENDIX A

Questions That Hamel Poses to Companies Regarding Principled Capitalism

PRINCIPLED
Capitalism degenerates into narrow self-interest without a strong ethical foundation.

- How do we focus the entire organization on a higher purpose and embed such virtues as generosity and selflessness into everyday interactions, evaluations, and reward systems?
- How do we measure the ethical or moral climate of a company, and what is the dashboard?
- What does it mean for individuals at all levels to act as wise stewards of organizational values, resources, and stakeholder well-being?
- What kind of a forum or process could we create that would allow individuals to freely share and discuss ethical dilemmas?
- In what ways might extreme transparency preserve and promote the highest purpose of the organization?

PATIENT
Vision and perseverance are critical to value creation—and highly vulnerable to short-termism.

- How do we stretch management timeframes and perspectives?
- What does it mean to articulate and instill a vision compelling enough to inspire sacrifice, stimulate innovation, and hedge against expediency?
- How might we rebalance compensation and measurement systems to provide incentives for long-term value creation along with short-term performance?
- What tactics or capabilities might we develop to earn some slack from investors?
- What kind of incentives and measurement systems could we devise to encourage internal entrepreneurs and nurture a varied portfolio of opportunities?

SOCIAL
Capitalism cannot operate in a social vacuum and profits and shareholder return can no longer be the only measures of a company's value-added.

- How do we eradicate the pervasive zero-sum mentality in business and embed the positive-sum view of stakeholder interdependence into operations at every level?
- How do we build the consideration of social return into every conversation and every decision at every level in the organization?
- How could we embed social goals into an organization's innovation agenda and processes? In other words, how might we encourage not just social responsibility, but social entrepreneurship?
- What kind of measurement and reward systems would give significant weight to the social impact created by individuals and the wider organization?

CHAPTER 2

STRATEGY IS LACKING

ABSTRACT

This chapter discusses some of the most glaring problems that academic institutions, and, more specifically, business programs, face today. Many have seen diminishing student enrollment and are unable to sustain the costs that have been escalating for several decades. In addition, most programs are very similar to one another, and minimal attempts have been made to differentiate them in any key ways.

Keywords: Strategic management, business models, differentiation, efficiencies

INTRODUCTION

Business programs theoretically train business students to be strategic thinkers who can develop and institute coherent, productive strategies. However, colleges and universities often fail to strategically manage their own business programs to provide the best "customer" value, namely, graduating students with the skills and education needed to thrive in the workplace. The following addresses how colleges and universities have often fallen short in providing this value to their "customers."

Stagnant Curricula

Business curricula in undergraduate and graduate business programs today often resemble curricula of the 1950s when business programs first grew in popularity. College administrators often steer towards a

A How-To Guide for Business School Practitioners, pp. 13–25

standardized curricula model to maintain a status quo with governmental and private accrediting bodies. In 2003 Doria et al. wrote:

> The current MBA education offered at most U.S. graduate business schools does not, in our view, adequately prepare people—even those attending the top schools—for the tougher-than-average challenges they will face when they start careers at leading corporations. Companies today demand good collaborative thinkers who cooperate to solve problems. Too often, schools deliver good analysts who compete to apply business-school formulas. Furthermore, companies demand specialized knowledge useful to particular professions. Schools, however, are more likely to deliver generalists who have trouble digging into special fields that can distinguish them and their employers. Companies demand leaders who can powerfully articulate ideas, orally and in writing, to motivate and guide their people. But schools tend to train people to simply assert their ideas; they don't sensitize them to the critical value of being an excellent communicator.

As Doria noted over 20 years ago, more frequent critiques of business schools at both the undergraduate and graduate levels focus on the lack of progress in preparing students for the market realities they will encounter after graduation. Denning (2018) points out that most business programs have utterly failed to keep up with the innovations and cultural changes that are transforming our society:

> As the world undergoes a Fourth Industrial Revolution that is "fundamentally altering the way we live, work and relate to one another—in its scale, scope, and complexity, a transformation... unlike anything humankind has experienced before"—one might imagine that business schools would be hotbeds of innovation and rethinking, with every professor keen to help understand and master this emerging new world. Paradoxically, it's the opposite. For the most part, today's business schools are busy teaching and researching 20th century management principles and, in effect, leading the parade towards yesterday.

Disjoint Between Education and Market Realities

According to Praxis.ets.org (n.d.), the College Learning Assessment Plus (CLA+) standardized test taken by freshmen and seniors at more than 200 colleges across the U.S. to measure how students' capabilities improved over the course of their studies, determined in its 2013–2016 study that "business majors make considerably fewer gains in critical thinking, analytical reasoning, and writing and communication than science, engineering, and math students, as well as liberal arts majors (history, literature, philosophy, etc.)." The site also reports that according to a PayScale survey, some 50% of employers feel that college graduates are not prepared for the workplace and listed their top complaints as follows:

- 60% of employers felt that critical thinking and problem-solving skills are lacking,
- 44% felt that graduates' writing proficiency is inadequate, and
- 39% felt that graduates lack public speaking skills (see Figure 2.1).

Figure 2.1

RECENT GRADUATES
LACK ESSENTIAL WORKPLACE SKILLS

 50 percent of employers feel that college graduates **aren't prepared for the workplace**

 44 percent of employers say that graduates' **writing proficiency is inadequate**

 60 percent of employers feel that **critical thinking and problem-solving skills** are lacking

 39 percent of employers say that graduates **lack public speaking skills**

Source: https://www.praxis.ets.com/about/say-care-and-future-workplace-review-2016-workforce-skills-preparedness-report

 PRAXIS

Although this study was conducted among a general population of college graduates, the report conveys that "the skills business graduates are failing to learn are almost an exact match for the valued skills that employers say graduates are lacking" (Praxis.ets.org, n.d.). Moreover, McGarry's (2018) study entitled *An Examination of Perceived Employability Skills between Employers and College Graduates* reinforces the findings regarding the gap between what employers expect of their new hires and what college graduates can offer.

The repeated ignoring of "customer" needs is proving detrimental to the profitability and viability of many business schools. Khurana, a Harvard professor, in a 2013 interview with Holstein, discussed the diminishing relevance of an MBA. He noted that "management school graduates are finding that their skills and training are not ideally matched to the needs of global corporations that have undergone rapid changes. Many of these companies are looking for business leaders who can help them expand in developing markets where the rules of engagement are quite different from what they might be at headquarters." John Benjamin, an MBA student and Dean's Fellow at the M.I.T. Sloan School of Management, concurs by noting that:

> MBA programs are not the open forums advertised in admissions bro-chures.... Business school instruction is routinely blinkered. An MBA class will consider a business issue ... in isolation. Its challenges are delineated; its society-level implications are waved away. The principals' overriding goal—profit maximization—is assumed. With mechanical efficiency, students then answer the question of how to move forward. Individual choices are ab-stracted into numbers or modeled as graph. (Denning, 2018)

Students also recognize that despite tolerating steep college tuition costs and accruing vast amounts of student loan debt, they are not pre-pared to take on the roles needed in the marketplace as employers convey (Bennett & Wilezol, 2013; Reynolds, 2012). Thus, traditional students are beginning to pursue alternatives to traditional degrees to be a better match in the marketplace, which, in turn, impacts colleges' profitability and ability to maintain or increase enrollments. This trend, coupled with the decreasing population of traditional college-age students, is exerting the negative financial pressure on colleges and universities that we dis-cussed in Chapter 1. This is especially true to those schools in the lower tiers with relatively small endowments.

Faculty Research Requirements

Ironically, another obstacle to innovation has been the growing trend towards additional faculty research requirements. Although faculty research is often touted as keeping faculty up-to-the-minute on everything happen-ing in the marketplace, the outcome is often the exact opposite. Faculty frequently carve out a narrow research specialty that enables them to immerse themselves in academic theory, dialogue only with other research-ers, and publish articles and books that actual business people will most likely never read.

Unfortunately, at most business schools, there is a much greater empha-sis on faculty performance through theoretical research than through active engagement with businesses (Bennis & O'Toole, 2005). This situation has widened the ever-growing divide between theory and practice, resulting in graduates who may lack exposure to the vocational perspective and remain ill-prepared for the realities of the business world. Chapter 4 fur-ther describes the detrimental impacts of this ever-widening divide and provides some suggestions for narrowing this gap.

Accrediting institutions, which raise and enforce curricular standards, have also played a part in the lack of innovation within business programs.

Too often, the application of accrediting standards results in the accredited programs replicating each other, which has led to widespread institutionalism, or the tendency for almost all programs to resemble each other very closely (DiMaggio & Powell, 1983). Denning (2018) acknowledges the stagnating role these accrediting institutions play when he argues, "The accreditation process of business schools guarantees glacial change to core curricula. It takes around five years to have even a small change in the core curriculum accepted by the accreditation process. (One highly successful Dean admits with frustration that 15 years of strenuous effort resulted in only two minor changes in the core curriculum)."

"College for All" Philosophy and Its Associated Problems

The historical movement of business programs to their current juncture is exacerbated by the widely popular sentiment in America that "every citizen deserves a college education." Unfortunately, this thinking has led to a system in which many students participate but either do not graduate with a degree or graduate with skills that are inadequate for the modern workplace (McGarry, 2018). According to Belkin (2020), "faith in the four-year degree traces back to the 1960s, when Civil Rights activists pushed for everyone to attend college and become a professional. Instead of steering students toward a pragmatic, though often racist and classist two-track system in which some high-school graduates headed to college and others became apprentices in a trade, the nation set a course for something more aspirational: college for all."

Thus, there has been a mass influx of college students with varying scholarly aptitude levels, with many of the most unprepared students gravitating toward business programs.

> At the undergraduate level, business schools do not enroll the very "best and brightest." Instead, gifted students—charmed by the critics of business education and persuaded that perhaps a graduate business degree will add earning potential that an undergraduate degree will not—are advised to choose liberal arts and science programs. Many bright students are discouraged from pursuing an undergraduate business degree as vocational and unbecoming of an intellectual. (Lorenzi, 2012)

Despite the diminishing relevance of business programs and the poor prospects for employment that students face upon graduation, many collegiate departments still fight to retain their traditional programming and systems. Many academics believe that new, innovative pedagogies and programs are trendy and faddish and that relying on them for financial returns will marginalize the importance of higher education. These concerns are understandable but fail to consider a dramatically changing economy. Of course, some trendy, "innovative" programs, such as Surf Science Technology and Adventure Education, may appear worthy of academic criticism. However, these contrast with the innovative programs that focus on the skills that employers seek, such as verbal and written communication, quantitative reasoning, and critical thinking.

Instead of actively seeking to create programs that better prepare business students for the workplace, many colleges and universities focus on accommodating the influx of students who may require additional support. For instance, colleges have added a plethora of student services, including remediation programs and academic tutoring, to assist underprepared students. Unfortunately, such services have increased overall collegiate expenses at a time when the target demographic is shrinking, admissions are falling, and tuition revenue is often declining. The failure to address these expenses and recognize how they undermine profitability exemplifies the anti-business bias prevalent at many colleges.

The Financial Cost of Supporting Students Who Are Not College-Ready

The movement to educate as many students as possible has precipitated college attendance among students who often need remediation in several academic subjects. Somewhere between 40% to 60% of first-year college students need remediation in English, math, or both, and on-time completion rates for students taking remedial classes are less than 10% (13 Upsetting Stats, 2021). Students enrolling in remediation classes often spend an extra semester or even an extra year on campus, which often includes additional costs and student loan debt.

Furthermore, offering a slew of remedial courses may not be in a college's best interest in terms of optimizing the use of its faculty, staff, budget, programs, and space. It may also not align with college mission statements that focus on fostering lifelong learning, liberal arts proficiency, and the development of critical thinking and analytical abilities. According to the American Academy of Arts and Sciences, in 2016, student support services at colleges and universities increased by 16% from 2002 to 2012. Similarly, the Delta Cost Project at the American Institutes for Research reviewed college spending patterns from 2001 to 2011 and found that the share of expenses devoted to student services rose from 17% of the average school's budget to 20% (Schoen, 2016). The Schoen report questions whether these student services are justifiable expenses or just additional "bloat."

A related expense for many colleges has been the burgeoning of support services for students who suffer from anxiety issues, learning disorders, or social disorientation. Colleges have responded by providing a plethora of services to assist and nurture these students. It deserves notice that some of these efforts have been tremendously and inspiringly successful. For example, a national survey by the Association for University and College Counseling Center Directors Annual Survey in 2018 found that 66% of college students felt counseling services improved their academic performance. Clearly, the expenses that student services require need to be incurred only when positive benefits can accrue to the educational institutions.

The Student Loan Threat to Financial Sustainability

Many of the current financial problems that colleges face can be directly linked to the reliance on student loans. Student loans have become so commonplace over the past 30 years (Bennett & Wilezol, 2013; Reynolds, 2012) that substantial and ever-increasing indebtedness has become interwoven with the college experience. The prevailing wisdom was that a college education would eventually create earning power that would justify these loans. Unfortunately, massive default rates have proven that this reasoning is often incorrect.

One out of every 10 Americans has defaulted on a student loan, and 7.8% of all student loan debt is in default (Hansen, 2021). Consequently, many political candidates contend that the country must remedy the high levels of student loan debt that many young American citizens currently carry. Ironically, many of these same politicians are the ones who initially voted for federal student loan programs that precipitated this "ballooning" debt in the first place.

The significant increases in the costs of a college education are largely enabled by the aggressive solicitation of the student loans that the government supports. Regarding the spike in tuition costs, a 2019 *Education Week* blog post noted that tuition at Stanford in 1972 was $2,850; this annual tuition rate had risen to $62,000 by 2019 (Sackstein, 2019). The blog continued to note that "according to the Bureau of Labor Statistics CPI Inflation Calculator, if Stanford tuition increased at the pace of overall inflation, it [the annual tuition] would be $17,007 today. That means that Stanford tuition has increased 3.64 times faster than general inflation. Other colleges are in the same boat more or less" (Sackstein, 2019).

Some colleges may view their higher tuitions as the cost for their "brand." However, another reality is that administrators typically do not seek out ways to better manage expenses. Instead, they have aimed to bring in more tuition and donor money to compensate for ever-increasing collegiate expenses. Through a whole panoply of student loans and grants, the

government for several decades has supported enrollments but simultaneously exacerbated the influx of students who are not college-ready—which,
in turn, results in colleges having to spend more money to accommodate
this student population. The illusion of governmental guarantees facilitates exorbitant borrowing, despite the questionable creditworthiness of
students and their forecasted ability to repay the loans after graduation.
Bennett and Wilezol (2013) summarize the economic dilemma that results
from the scenario:

> The truth is that too many people are going to college. Too many students
> are studying irrelevant material that leaves them ill-equipped for the job
> market. Too many students are paying too much for tuition and are left
> holding massive amounts of debt. Too many students are going to college
> and doing little other than indulging their own pastimes, partying, and
> hooking up.

Administrative complacency regarding the profit motive has significantly exacerbated financial conditions at many colleges and universities,
resulting in layoffs, hiring freezes, program cutting, and suspended contributions to employees' retirement funds. Some institutions have come
to rely upon their endowment funds to cover operating expenses. Two
dramatic predictions regarding the fate of academic institutions have been
widely publicized in the media with varying degrees of support and dis-
sent. Michael Horn (2018), who studies education at Harvard University,
predicts that 25% of schools will fail in the next two decades, and Clayton
Christensen, a Harvard business professor, has repeatedly projected that
50% of the 4,000 colleges and universities in the U.S. will be bankrupt in
10 to 15 years. Although these are dramatic forecasts, there is no question
that administrators need to perform their tasks in a more business-oriented
manner if their programs and colleges are to survive and thrive.

In order to reduce their mounting tuition rates, administrators need to
cut operational expenses and strategically focus on balancing the budget,
which is overlooked at many institutions. Although collegiate budgetary
frugality has never been more necessary, many colleges believe they have to
offer a slew of high-priced amenities in order to boost enrollment. Newlon
(2014) highlights a free movie theater, a 25-person hot tub and spa with a
lazy river and whirlpool, a leisure pool with biometric hand scanners for
secure entry, a 50-foot climbing wall, and a top-of-the-line steak restaurant
with free five-course meals as just some of the amenities offered at college
campuses to appeal to a contemporary student body. This whole cycle feeds
on itself: High-priced tuitions facilitate growth in student amenities, which
colleges often use as a "bidding war" to attract students. Significantly, these
amenities are often unrelated to student academic success and may serve
as a distraction from student learning.

The Proliferation of Amenities Breaking the Bank

The proliferation of "bonus" student amenities began about a decade ago, at the same time that large numbers of "millennials" began selecting colleges. Many of the members of this generational cohort had come of age in small families that enjoyed a high standard of living and were raised in comfortable conditions (Newlon, 2014). Colleges and universities recognized that this population and their parents expected their prospective institutions to reproduce the more lavish living conditions that the students enjoyed at home. Consequently, dorms were often reconfigured and rebuilt to resemble hotels, and amenities foreign to the general population one generation prior became standard features on many college campuses.

In her 2019 dissertation, Lucinda Sue McDonald cites Suttell's report on a 2007 conference for higher education professionals entitled, "The Campus of the Future: A Meeting of the Minds." McDonald (2019) highlights several key takeaways from this conference regarding the increasing demands of contemporary college students as follows:

- Facilities play a supporting role in attracting and retaining students.
- The campus and facilities have become the face of the institution, and if students don't like them, they will leave.
- 26–27% of students attend a school because they like the campus, not the programs.
- Traditional students (age 18–22) today want more [in the way of amenities] than in years past; they are more discriminating and have higher expectations for comfort, campus-wide.
- Students often compare colleges based on "the best technology, the best buildings, and the best on-campus eateries."

Not surprisingly, as the demand for such amenities grows, so too does the cost of the entire college experience. On many college campuses, the focus has shifted from competitive academic growth to accommodating extravagant lifestyle demands. These demands have become extensive and fuel the already skyrocketing tuition costs at colleges and universities.

Mismanagement of Academic Programs

Instead of focusing on the value of programs for the student consumer, administrators often focus on promoting the academic research of colleagues, which militates against generating profit and balancing budgets in several ways. First, teaching the communication skills that students need to be competitive in the workplace is often ignored. Second, students often do not receive the technical training in quantitative literacy or technology needed to thrive in the workplace. Finally, by emphasizing theoretical research as a criterion for tenure, administrators inadvertently encourage business faculty to shift their priorities away from real-world business, thus making them unable to advise students effectively.

Prioritizing the theoretical over the practical is perhaps a luxury that colleges can no longer afford. The need to remedy this situation has never been more pressing because, as Rao (2015) points out, "the pendulum is swinging again, and the golden age of business academic research is coming to an end. Deans will need to have two skills that billion-dollar entrepreneurs have—the ability to get revenues and the ability to control cash flow. Inexperienced program administrators are no longer able to satisfy the expectations of consumers."

Although many college administrators are often highly paid, many in high-ranking business program positions are often inexperienced in financial matters (Rao, 2015). They also tend to have limited skills regarding the strategic planning process. The reason for these shortcomings is that these jobs are often considered rewards or perks; senior career faculty are often selected for these critically important positions, despite a competitive environment that demands business acumen. Further, the performance metrics used to measure administrative achievement at colleges are much vaguer than in the private sector, and the resulting lack of accountability provides a framework in which poor decision-making may occur.

Much of the growth in the number of college administrators has occurred in order to manage remediation programs, which are needed to position underprepared students for academic achievement. Moreover, additional administrators are needed to meet the increased reporting requirements imposed by the federal and state governments and accrediting bodies, which indicates a shift towards bureaucratic control as opposed to consumer-oriented action on the part of colleges and universities.

Between 1993 and 2007, the number of full-time administrators per 100 students at America's leading universities grew by 39%, while the number of employees engaged in teaching, research, or service grew by 18% (Bennett & Wilezol, 2013). This increase in administration is concerning because most students do not directly benefit from growth in this area. This administrative hiring "bloat" reached its apex in 2013 when the number of traditional-aged college students in the population began to shrink. While students and their parents prioritize schools that employ experienced, knowledgeable professors, colleges, and universities, often place less emphasis on this crucial piece of the collegiate experience.

Another significant financial burden is imposed when institutions must support highly paid tenured professors with reduced course loads who may only teach classes on abstruse subjects aligned with their research. Moreover, these faculty members may provide limited support for their students, departments, and colleges. Since most highly credentialed faculty generally do not teach core or lower-level classes in their disciplines, colleges often have to incur the cost of hiring adjuncts or junior faculty to cover much of the work that was traditionally relegated to all faculty.

Moreover, there is a lack of expectation for faculty participation in activities or standard operating procedures that would promote programs and assist colleges in operating in a more financially sound manner. For example, many faculty are unwilling to participate in value-added programs for students because they do not view such activities as part of their job description. If faculty choose not to teach core or intro courses and select classes with smaller enrollments, perhaps some type of merit-based criterion is needed to demonstrate that faculty are indeed contributing to their departments and institutions.

Prospective students and parents also demand to see the employment prospects that they can expect upon graduation before contracting with colleges for large sums of money. Unfortunately, much of the data regarding after-graduation job placement is grim. A recent report from Burning Glass Technologies found that underemployment is a pervasive problem among college graduates.

> Each year, one of every five graduates who walks across the stage at commencement to collect a diploma is a business major, making it far and away the most popular undergraduate major. Business majors are generally more likely to be underemployed than average (47% for business vs. 43% overall). (Burning Glass, 2018)

Thus, college administrators can no longer focus on factors that are peripheral to the needs of students, such as publishing "scholarly" works for an audience of academics, supporting underperforming programs, and spending time incorporating a politically correct agenda into their offerings. If business schools are to survive as a respected training front, they will need to pay more careful attention to the demands of their stakeholders, including a discerning student population and employers with evolving needs.

REFERENCES

Association for University and College Counseling Center Directors Annual Survey—Public Version (2018). https://www.aucccd.org/assets/documents/Survey/2018%20AUCCCD%20Survey-Public-June%2012-FINAL.pdf

16 Upsetting facts about college remediation rates. What to become. (2023). https://whattobecome.com/blog/college-remediation-rates/

Belkin, D. (2022, July 20). Broke colleges resort to mergers for survival. *The Wall Street Journal*. https://www.wsj.com/articles/broke-colleges-resort-to-mergers-for-survival-11658239445

Bennett, W., & Wilezol, D. (2013). *Is college worth it?* Thomas Nelson.

Bennis, W., & O'Toole, J. (2005, May). How business schools lost their way. *Harvard Business Review;* https://hbr.org/2005/05/how-business-schools-lost-their-way

Burning Glass Technologies. (2018). *Majors that matter: Ensuring college graduates avoid unemployment*. Retrieved January 23, 2021, https://www.burning-glass.com/wpcontent/uploads/underemployment_majors_that_matter_final.pdf

Denning, S. (2018, May 27). Why today's business schools teach yesterday's expertise. *Forbes*. https://www.forbes.com/sites/stevedenning/2018/05/27/why-todays-business-schools-teach-yesterdays-expertise/?sh=6805d701488b

Dimaggio P., & Powell, W. (1983). The iron cage revisited: Institutional isomorphism and collective rationality in organizational fields. *American Sociological Review, 48*, 147–160.

Doria, J., Rozanski, H., & Cohen, E. (2003, Fall). What business needs from business schools. *Leadership, 32*. https://www.strategy-business.com/article/03305

Hansen, M. (2021). Student loan default rate. *Education Data Initiative*. https://educationdata.org/student-loan-defaultrate#:~:text=An%20average%20of%2015%25%20of,is%20in%20defaulted%20student%20loans

Horn, M. (2018). Will half of all colleges really close in the next decade? *Forbes*. https://www.forbes.com/sites/michaelhorn/2018/12/13/will-half-of-all-colleges-really-close-in-the-next-decade/?sh=38c7b34f52e5

Lorenzi, P. Business Schools: Capitalism's Last Stand. Soc 49, 230–239 (2012). https://doi.org/10.1007/s12115-012-9536-x

McDonald, L. S. (2019). *The impact of campus facilities on the recruitment of students in higher education* [Western Kentucky University Dissertation]. https://digitalcommons.wku.edu/cgi/viewcontent.cgi?article=1169&context=diss

McGarry, K. (2018, April 3). The skills gap: Employers expect more than what college grads offer. *The James G. Martin Center for Academic Renewal*. https://www.jamesgmartin.center/2018/04/skills-gap-employers-expect-college-grads-offer/

Newlon, C. (2014). The college amenities "Amenities Arms Race" in higher education 143 arms race. *Forbes*. https://www.forbes.com/sites/caranewlon/2014/07/31/the-collegeamenitiesarms-race/#437c70c54883

Praxis.ets.org. (n.d.). *Is a business degree worth it?* https://discoverpraxis.com/13002/is-a-businessdegree-worth-it/ https://discoverpraxis.com/blog/13002/is-a-business-degree-worth-it#:~:text=96%25%20of%20Praxis%20graduates%20are,Praxis%20participants%20is%20%2450K

Rao, D. (2015, May 2). Should business school deans know real business? *Forbes*. https://www.forbes.com/sites/dileeprao/2015/03/02/should-business-school-deans-know-real-business/?sh=e8d2796364bb

Reynolds, G. (2012). *The higher education bubble*. Encounter Books.

Sackstein, S. (2019, April 18). Why has the cost of college outpaced inflation? *Education Week Teacher.* https://www.edweek.org/teaching-learning/opinion-why-has-the-cost-of-college-outpaced-inflation/2019/04

Schoen, J. (2016). *Why does a college degree cost so much?* Retrieved January 13, 2021, https://www.cnbc.com/2015/06/16/why-college-costs-are-so-high-and-rising.html

CHAPTER 3

CREATING VALUE FOR CONSUMERS BY RESPECTING BUSINESS PRINCIPLES

ABSTRACT

This chapter explores the causes of several glaring problems faced by academic institutions and their business schools. It also puts forth some solutions to address some of the issues faced such as stagnant curricula, poor student preparation for the real-world and out of touch administrators.

Keywords: business school curricula, college administrators, customer value, differentiation

INTRODUCTION

In this chapter, we discuss some of the macro problems that are currently facing many business schools, and what colleges and university administrators might do to remedy some of them. In later chapters, we address some of the micro problems that are related to business school curricula. The authors provide suggestions for improvement and relay strategies that they have relied upon during their academic careers.

Outdated Curricula and Research Focus

As mentioned in earlier chapters, business program curricula resemble each other at most schools, largely due to the requirements of accrediting

A How-To Guide for Business School Practitioners, pp. 27–48
Copyright © 2024 by Information Age Publishing
www.infoagepub.com

bodies and the mimetic practices that these institutions employ in their benchmarking. Many small and medium-sized colleges were established as teaching colleges, leaving the research to the larger, better-endowed or taxpayer-funded institutions. In recent years, however, in trying to achieve prominence through faculty publications, many of these smaller schools have offered their faculty generous perks such as course release time to pursue research agendas that are often unrelated to anything that would enrich a business or accounting curricula. This, once again, represents a lack of foresight on the part of administrators, as the model was never one that could be sustained in the long term.

It is widely recognized through homogenous hiring and promotion processes that business schools reward empirical and statistically validated research (Bennis & O'Toole, 2005; Rao, 2015) whether or not the research is helpful to students or businesses. Whereas many large, well-endowed universities have the resources and the research budgets to fund large amounts of faculty research and release time from teaching, most small colleges simply do not. These practices have also served to erode differentiation among schools. Almost all accredited academic institutions reward the same performance among their faculty and do not work to focus on any practices that might serve to distinguish their graduates from those of other competing institutions. Because of this, students (and their parents) often gravitate to the school that will provide the greatest discount, as opposed to the one that will enrich their life the most in the pursuit of their future goals.

The inefficiency of the current system has only recently been discussed. DeCosta-Klipa (2019) quotes Michael Horn, an author and education consultant who says that many colleges "are structured to be the opposite of efficient with low teacher-to-student ratios, expanding support services, faculty members with low productivity and generous benefit packages." In addition, unrealistic promotion and tenure practices serve to diminish productivity. These measures, which have been undertaken by nearly every academic institution, have served to drain financial resources and, in addition, use these resources in ways that do not serve to differentiate the institutions in any novel way that might bring about a competitive advantage.

The divide between the real-world and the academic cocoon is widening as indicated by the fact that "today it is possible to find tenured professors of management who have never set foot inside real business, except as customers" (Bennis & O'Toole, 2005). Denning (2018) also notes this lack of management experience and the relationship to business school atrophy. Business schools are not only burdened with administrators who are out of touch with contemporary business (or any business, for that matter) but have increasingly become filled with complacent faculty as well.

Not Prepared to Follow, Manage, or Lead

Complacency in administrative matters and dictates from accrediting bodies has left the curricula and operations at most business schools basically the same as they have been since the 1950s, despite radical transformations in almost every aspect of the business world (Rao, 2015).

The lack of initiative on the part of many business school administrators and faculty has also led to their not teaching their students several of the most necessary skills in business—how to follow, manage, and lead. In all three cases, preparing students for success in the business world depends upon putting them in touch with reality—along with theory—and giving them the opportunity to apply what they learn and to practice applying their knowledge and skills. As Henry Mintzberg, a noted scholar on management issues, laments, "MBA programs not only fail to develop managers but give their students a false impression of managing that, when put into practice, is undermining our organizations and our societies" (Mintzberg, 2005).

In Mintzberg's book, *Managers not MBAs* (2005), he expresses his doubts that business schools can graduate exceptional 21st-century managers based on a program first introduced in 1908 and not revised since the late 1950s. According to Mintzberg,

> We don't need heroes in positions of influence any more than technocrats. We need balanced, dedicated people who practice a style of managing that can be called engaging. Such people believe that their purpose is to leave behind stronger organizations, not just higher share prices. They do not display hubris in the name of leadership.

Mintzberg sees problems in business that are resultant from the focus on quantitative matters rather than human problems. The MBA programs that he discusses often use case analyzes in their teaching and Mintzberg finds that in this way the experiences of the student are widely separated from actual business activities. In Chapter 4, we further discuss the schism between the scholarly and the applied and in Chapter 5 we elaborate on the practice of service-learning as a pedagogy that can address the problem that Mintzberg highlights.

In our experience, the basic requirements that are most deficient in the preparation of business school graduates are:

- effective communication skills,
- the understanding and application of ethical principles,
- decision-making abilities, and
- quantitative reasoning skills.

- In later chapters, we will discuss ways in which business programs might improve students' skills and abilities in these areas.

Anti-Capitalist Bias in Business Schools

In addition to the lack of experience in actual businesses and their lack of interest in teaching students how to thrive in such an environment, some of the complacency that afflicts many business school administrators and faculty seems to derive from the low opinion in which many of them hold business itself. It seems counterintuitive that administrators and faculty would choose business as their field of interest, study it for years, teach it, and administer programs in business when they fundamentally do not admire free enterprise and actually mischaracterize it to their students and teach them to have contempt for many business practices. Much of the blame for company failures and ethical lapses at many high-profile firms has been placed by the business press on the business schools that prepared corrupt managers for their work. Jacobs (2009), a professor at University of North Carolina's Kenan-Flagler Business School writes that:

> By failing to teach the principles of corporate governance and account-ability, B-school graduates have matured into executives and investment bankers who have failed American workers and retirees, many of whom have witnessed their jobs and savings vanish. Most B-schools paper over the topic by requiring first-year students to take a compulsory ethics class, which is necessary, but not sufficient.

Jacobs also asks cynically, "Would Bernie Madoff have acted differently if he had aced his ethics final?"

Another common critique that has been directed at the schools is that they turned out graduates who are experts in quantitative analysis but were are less articulate about human needs. These students are often experts in numbers, data, and technical research, but sadly lacking in either knowing how to apply this information ethically, or sadly lacking in the courage to do the right thing. In recent years, we have also witnessed an erosion in quantitative abilities in addition to the inability to recognize an ethical issue, further weakening the value of these students to industry. With regard to the laxity in the area of ethics it is important to note that students need at least two areas of "expertise"—first, they need to know what is right—what the principles are and why they exist and how they conduce to human happiness and business success—and, second, the students need to have cultivated the prudence, justice, temperance, and courage to do the right thing—especially in difficult situations. In Chapter 8, we discuss the teaching of these four Aristotelian cardinal virtues (later adopted by Christians) and giving students the opportunity to practice and apply them.

Business School Reaction to Criticisms

It is instructive to note how most business schools have reacted to these criticisms leveled against them. Some schools have done well and profited from their response to market forces, developing innovative programming and providing novel learning opportunities to their students.

For example, Northeastern University has made a name for itself through its high-profile internship and cooperative education programs. *U.S. News & World Report* (2023) "ranked programs at universities and colleges that offer well-regarded study abroad, service learning and other special programs that, research shows, are linked to student success and positive learning outcomes while fostering a successful undergraduate student experience." Northeastern University ranked first in this category. Their program requires their co-op students to take a preparation course to learn resume writing, interviewing skills, workplace etiquette and other topics. Before participating in their first co-op, which takes place the second semester of sophomore year or the summer after, students must meet with their co-op coordinator. Interestingly, this school beats out other preeminent institutions in this category, including MIT (ranked 7th), Cornell (10), Stanford (14), Harvard (19-tie) and University of Notre Dame (19-tie). The prospect of putting students to work and gaining active knowledge about the business world is appealing to many prospective students and their families and combats what many feel is a divide between theory and application.

Most business schools, however, in response to the growing negative sentiment against them, have begun to de-emphasize profitability and, in many cases, to vilify capitalists. Students are frequently taught that capitalism is primarily responsible for many of society's problems. Significantly, those who offer such across-the-board criticisms do not usually suggest any alternative economic systems that provide better solutions. Capitalism is rarely presented as a system that can continue to improve lives and enrich humanitarian activity. Sheeran (2000) writes that the terms "social, ethical, and environmental responsibility" in the context of management education "have nothing to do with a fair-minded empirical analysis of business and society. Rather, these terms are code words for antibusiness propaganda, junk science and anti-technology bias. The purpose of such courses is to undermine the moral legitimacy of business and to persuade future business managers of the urgent need for more regulatory restrictions on economic freedom." This is unfortunate because, as Novak (1996) has highlighted, when principled free enterprise works as it should, morality and capitalism align with each other.

As Yonk and Simmons (2017) note:

> Business education teaches entrepreneurship and ethics as fragmented, narrow disciplines, and capitalism as amoral or even immoral. This approach produces students and business leaders with a misunderstanding of what it means to be engaged in business. Too often, we find business leaders either apologetic for their success, complacent or engaged in fraudulent behavior.

Similarly, contemporary literature and Hollywood films also often vilify capitalism, as do some groups of highly profiled politicians who take it for granted that all big businesses are corrupt. It has become commonplace for students to be conditioned toward anti-capitalist views in the general education courses that they take prior to or concurrent with their business curricula. Worthen (2022) in reporting a *New York Times* opinion piece about the changing focus of business schools away from capitalist initiatives writes that "After decades of emphasis on financial markets and shareholder returns, business schools are trying to take on deeper philosophical problems—including, maybe, tentative questions about the means and ends of capitalism itself." 'She continues that "even before the pandemic, business schools were offering initiatives and 'program concentrations' with names like 'Conscientious Capitalism' and 'Sustainable Business.'" It appears that all too often, a primary objective of such classes is to denigrate the free market system to students.

Business students are repeatedly exposed to the case studies of firms such as Enron, BP, and Tyco, where ethical grounding was completely compromised at the expense of illegal profits. These examples are good in that they alert students to these cases and to the failure of the system and of the safeguards meant to prevent such disasters from arising. Equally, if not more important, however, are the messages that business programs communicate as to how to prevent such situations from occurring. The solution presented to the students by professors is often increased government oversight, which would restrict free market operations, add another layer of bureaucracy, cost the business, the consumer, and the taxpayer more money, and not necessarily succeed in preventing such failures in the future. Such "solutions" do not get to the heart of the problem because they often neglect the role that the sound, moral judgment of managers and their supervisors should and could have played. Frequently, professors who prefer to encourage further government controls ignore principled capitalism's ability to serve as a self-correcting system. In fact, it was the application of such capitalist principles that brought these firms to their demise as a direct consequence of their wrongdoings.

Related to universities' attempts to squash capitalist values, professors often teach "social responsibility" in a way that favors wealth redistribution over wealth creation. This type of focus serves to diminish the powerful role that capitalism can play in serving diverse societal needs—such as preparing students to help their fellow citizens and the society at large through their wealth creation and hiring practices. Under such exalted, essentially socialist philosophies, obligations are to be fulfilled from the top-down, instead of through a participatory, democratic economic system that benefits all.

It certainly seems likely that the professoriate's tendency to shun capitalist ideals also impacts administrative practices in ways that are detrimental to the profit margins of schools. Worthen's (2022) article on the changing goals of business educators highlights the anti-free-market leanings when he cites Brian Lowery, a professor at the Stanford Graduate School of Business. Lowery is enthused that, in academia, "There's been a little tempering of the fervor for laissez-faire capitalism.... There's healthy conversation about that," said Lowery, who recently taught a course entitled "Reimagining Work Post-Covid."

Consumer Enlightenment

Consumers and employers have become more active in their response to the changing educational focus and the diminishing returns that students are experiencing in the market upon graduation. In fact, the requirements for participation in many business sectors seem to be shifting away from the requirement of a college degree, and this is complicating college recruitment efforts. In a sector where tuition rates far outpaced inflation rates for many years and were not met with a negative consumer response, there now appears to be some market forces at work. The business schools' lack of responsiveness to students, parents, employers, and market forces have encouraged those stakeholders to take their business elsewhere—which, in turn, will make it even harder for many business schools to make a profit. In addition, many employers are backing off from hiring expensive business school graduates whom they are often dissatisfied with. For example, Hess and Addison (2018) cite a 2017 Harvard Business School study that found that "college graduates filling middle-skill positions cost more to employ, have higher turnover rates, tend to be less engaged, and are no more productive than high-school graduates doing the same job."

Consequently, many companies are seeking non-degreed workers who come at a much lower price, are more engaged, and are willing to be trained to meet specific company needs. In 2018, Glassdoor compiled a list of 15 major U.S. companies that no longer require applicants to have a college degree for many entry and mid-level jobs. The companies include Apple, Google, Costco, Home Depot, and Bank of America. Hess and Addison (2018) note that colleges have reaped the "outsize benefits of acting as the gatekeepers to employment. It is an arrangement which allows campus bureaucrats to pull in six-figure salaries while tuition costs soar ever-higher and schools feast on billions in federal student loans and other taxpayer funds."

This move on the part of the private corporations threatens business schools and provides a window into public sentiment toward academic institutions. These same large corporations sharply cut back on funding of MBA programs following the 2008 recession (Rao, 2015). Former President Donald Trump furthered the pressure on academic institutions in June 2020, when he signed an executive order that required the federal personnel management office to revise the required qualifications for jobs with the U.S. government. Under this order, a college degree will be required only if mandated by law, or if agencies filling a position believe such a degree is necessary. This puts college standards and the value to employers under additional scrutiny.

An esteemed colleague once extolled that, "A college can train students to go around all day quoting Horatio but, at the end of the day, if the college does not prepare students for meaningful work, it has not done its job." The breadth that a rigorous college education provides is invaluable, but if college business programs do not develop workplace skills, consumers will eventually reject those programs—a process that has already begun in the private and public sectors. The future of many U.S. business schools is under threat unless their programs can become more relevant to the needs of employers. It is becoming more obvious that to counter the private and public sector movements away from the college degree requirement, business schools must upgrade and improve their practices regarding curricula, delivery modes, hiring policies and standards if they are to survive and flourish.

The challenge for administrators and faculty is to adjust current systems and, in some cases, to make radical alterations to these systems. These systemic alterations need to modify programs so that students will be able to demonstrate the broader skills that employers are now demanding of graduates. Static systems that respond to the requirements of accrediting agencies, as well as the professional training for faculty and requirements for faculty selection, are all proving inappropriate in the midst of radical societal changes. As Friga et al. (2003) argue, "Given the relationship between management education and the business world, market forces such as globalization, technological change, and new workplace requirements may affect business education more than any other discipline in academia."

Standardized curricula and programs prompted U.S. Senator Ben Sasse, the former president of Midland Lutheran college (now Midland University) in Nebraska, to write in 2019 that one of the striking aspects of the college search process for his daughter was:

> how similarly many schools seek to present themselves—and how few make any clear promises about how our daughter would be changed, improved, better habituated, or made more thoughtful by investing four of her most valuable years in their care.

In addition to differentiation, program administrators need to develop a selection process that can locate and attract the most beneficial hires to train their students. In Chapter 4, we discuss some of the faculty requirements that may serve students and employers better than those which are typical for the profession. We discuss professional tracks as supportive of tenured academic tracks and encourage practitioner activity to complement academic. Faculty are those who are on the front line with consumers and on whom much of a program's success depends. They should be competent, well-educated people of integrity and common sense, who can demonstrate how to apply theoretical knowledge, and who can successfully coach students to do this as well. Business program administrators should also seek to employ intelligent practitioners who have experienced success in the workplace and who understand and are able to model the fundamentals of following, working on a team, managing, and leading.

The global pandemic of 2020 has altered the higher education landscape in many ways and has highlighted some of the deficiencies in business programs. The admission and financial pressures that the COVID pandemic has put on schools has made innovation, upgrading, and customer-responsiveness more important than ever before. We highlight below some ways that we think that administrators and faculties of business programs can provide value to students and employers in the coming years.

SOME PROPOSED SOLUTIONS

Encouraging Disciplined Strategic Thinking

Academic business programs can learn from successful businesses in that they need to have a worthwhile product and to carve a particular "niche" in the market. To that end, they must develop their offerings to be distinct and must provide value for consumers that competing academic institutions may not have the competencies to provide. Lapovsky (2018), a personal finance reporter for *Forbes* writes:

Historically, many of us advised institutions to "stay in their lane," meaning that they should stick with their mission no matter how narrowly defined. The advice was just to execute better on what you were good at doing. Today, I think most colleges with narrowly defined mission statements, especially those which are primarily undergraduate liberal arts institutions, need to think very seriously about moving outside their lanes.

This advice certainly pertains to programs in management education. Many critics agree with Laponsky's argument that colleges need to think about both reforming the curriculum and changing instructional methods (Bennett & Wilezol, 2013; Reynolds, 2012). Curricula should emphasize the development of problem-solving and conceptual abilities with the goal of preparing students to be ethical, strong-minded members of society. Some of the suggested curricula reforms that we believe can be helpful are highlighted in Chapters 5–8 of this book.

Bennett and Wilezol (2013) repeatedly refer to a "bubble" when explaining the ever-expanding demand for a commodity that is diminishing in value and increasing in price. This "bubble" has begun to burst and post-bubble, "students are likely to be far more concerned about getting actual value for their educational dollars" (Reynolds, 2012). Due to the aforementioned issues, it has never been more important for college business administrators to think and act strategically. For example, programs should be unique to a college or university's strengths, perhaps in a particular geography or because of a specific corporate partner and their needs.

Results-Oriented Assessment for College Administrators

In addition to a lack of fit between programming and school core competencies, schools and programs often hire administrators whose proficiencies are very loosely related to the college or program's core missions. These individuals often come at a high cost that puts a burden on the execution of programs. Many programs that do not address career preparation skills are being run with huge administrative costs. Consequently, perhaps administrators should be "graded" at least in part on how well and frequently they eliminate programs that are not academically important, attractive to students, or successful in preparing students for the marketplace. Bennett and Wilezol (2013) suggests, for example, that "colleges should think hard about eliminating trendy majors that consistently do not demonstrate their intellectual rigor, fiduciary worth, or ability to produce employable graduates." Some noteworthy, trendy majors that do not appear to offer students much value either in school or afterwards include The Beatles, The Bowling Industry, Surf Studies and Leisure Studies (UofPeople, 2023). Despite the many administrative hurdles to eliminating a minor, a major, a program—or even a course, decisions to do so must be addressed in a financially astute, timely, and well-conceived manner.

In addition, administrator performance should be assessed both quantitatively and qualitatively as is done in the private sector. It is difficult to make judgments about performance in the way that many schools currently operate because of the qualitative and often highly subjective rating systems. Often, in academic programs, assessments are less formal than in the private sector and abstract standards that are not quantifiable are commented upon. When quantification is attempted, archaic standards are often utilized such as numbers of citations of an article or number of campus events attended. In our experience, we have seen reviews conducted that do not rely on explicit standards and are not specifically results-oriented. Most assessments of administrators are not, as in business, tightly based on a risk/benefit calculation and therefore, most academic administrators are not faced with the up-or-out culture that exists in many businesses. In order to implement these type of business assessment models, colleges would have to move from a superficially "collegial" culture to one that is more merit-based. As a result of the assessment systems in place, administrators often stay in their positions for years, despite failing programs and revenue losses. This problem also often occurs with senior faculty members who become more and more entrenched in their positions and generate less and less value for their students, their junior colleagues, their departments, and their colleges. In addition to profitability metrics that can be tied to programs, assessment measures should be tied to graduate performance as well as alumni donations and feedback. These factors certainly can be indicative of program profitability. These same factors could be also used strategically to assess faculty performance.

Faculty members who want to be promoted, make more money, or who wish to scale back on teaching often transition to administrative roles in business schools. The administrative abilities of these faculty, even if their motivations are pure, may not be suitable for achieving programmatic innovation and advancement. Although colleges should certainly be willing to consider internal candidates, they should recognize that external candidates can often be much more effective administrators for numerous reasons. First, candidates with a proven record of administrative success should ordinarily be preferred to candidates who may have some aptitude in such an area but have not had any proven track record in it. Second, if a program or department needs to be turned around, it is much more likely that an external candidate can succeed in making the necessary changes. A candidate who has taught in the department for years and who has all kinds of friendships, alliances, and connections may not be able to make the changes necessary to streamline a department or to improve programs—especially when this involves cutting jobs, programs, or budgets. Strategic position descriptions should be designed—that spell out educational credentials, teaching experience, and real-world background in the field. The candidates should also be asked for a record of having successfully demonstrated the actual aptitudes required for the job. Selection committees should be carefully trained concerning the necessary criteria for the job and need to do interviews in which almost all the questions ask candidates to demonstrate the reasoning, strategic thinking, communication abilities, and problem-solving skills that he or she will need to be successful. It goes without saying that administrative candidates should possess the credentials that best suit the program. However, such key positions should not be viewed as rewards for longevity or as part-time posts that are peripheral to teaching but should be viewed as critically important functions that can guide the programs to higher levels of performance and profitability.

Retooled selection and assessment programs for college administrators are necessary at many institutions, as are those for college faculty members. Many faculty members do not themselves think or act strategically; many of them do not operate within the budgets allocated to them; and many of them have what could charitably be called "insouciance" concerning whether or not their department or their college operates in the black—so long as they get paid, and their own programs and perks are not affected. Perhaps these faculty members might be incentivized in order to keep up with what is going on in the real world of business, to extending their networks to include managers and others in various businesses, and upgrading the faculty's own business and advising skills so that what they teach, the way they teach it, what they model, and their own advising are more up-to-speed and up-to-date. The changes that are done with regard to administrators will not have an impact if appropriate changes to faculty assessment and training programs are not instituted, including changes to what is required for tenure in a business department.

Collaborating With Private and Public Partners

The linkages between real-world operations and what goes on in the college business program can extend to private-public partnerships. Just as many private businesses engage in strategic alliances to quickly tap into market demands, collegiate business programs should do the same. In the past, these types of strategic alliances were considered too far outside of any college's mission. Northeastern University, in contrast, is thriving based upon the work-study model that it was built upon a century ago. "Today, its students intern at one of 3,100 companies during their education. That forces professors to adjust their curricula repeatedly to meet the needs of industry" (Belkin, 2022).

Despite a laissez-faire attitude toward these types of alliances at many institutions, they appear to offer an opportunity for beneficial branding and increased revenue opportunities. Lapovsky (2018) notes that "among the cost saving initiatives with the greatest potential will be collaborative activities among institutions and with new partners, public and private even including mergers in some cases as well as the de-siloing of institutions." For example, Marist College in Poughkeepsie recently announced that it was building a medical school with Nuvance, the largest healthcare provider in its geographic locale. Metropolitan State University in Denver has also partnered with Sage Hospitality to open a chain hotel (Metropolitan State University, 2018). These projects are novel but appear to be slow to get up and running despite the promise that they hold productive, mutually beneficial alliances.

Launching Academically Enriching Programs That Prepare Students for Diverse Careers

As we discussed in Chapter 2, employers are looking for several skills and dispositions in the individuals that they hire: excellent communication skills, solid quantitative reasoning abilities, sound decision-making and high ethical ideals are repeatedly cited. Willingness to take initiative, to take direction, to work as a team; to take responsibility, and to be held accountable are often also mentioned. Business schools are frequently criticized for teaching students largely in technical areas and ignoring these requirements and other applied skills, including risk management, internal governance, behavior of complex systems, regulation and business/government regulations and socially responsible leadership (Barrett, 2010).

In addition, business programs are also castigated for failing to deliver students of sound moral character. In 2010, the dean of the University of Chicago Booth School of Business touched on a related subject—the need to teach students to question and to be willing to disagree with their professors in pursuit of the truth. He said that the "most important change needed was not new curricular materials or courses but faculty and student behaviors that encouraged deep questioning and professional communication without trading substance for deference" (Datar et al., 2010). Business programs that focus on remedying these deficiencies have the opportunity to stand out among their competitors.

A Return to Teaching About Capitalist Virtues

One of the greatest opportunities business programs have nationwide is to represent principled capitalism fairly, to describe its historical successes, and to focus on the local, national, and international ways in which free-enterprise systems, if properly regulated and operated, have benefited millions of individuals, as well as whole countries and societies. An under-reported, but ongoing trend that we believe represents one of the greatest lapses in many modern business programs is the devaluation and misrepresentation of the principled free-market system. Although it is necessary and appropriate to criticize the failures of capitalism as a system and to hold companies and individual free marketers to account for their misdeeds, many administrators and faculty members in business programs act as if free-market economics and the associated capitalist system were the parents of virtually all modern evils. It is a mystery as to why administrators and faculty who think so poorly of the free-enterprise system have devoted their lives to teaching or managing programs about it. Also mystifying is why they would think that students would be attracted in great numbers to a field that those who teach it themselves hold in such disdain.

The full truth about the principled free-enterprise system is an exciting, even inspiring story. Faculty and administrators who are willing to tell that story clearly and fairly will attract students to their field, excite them about their major, and help them to be enthusiastic about their chosen vocation. Students who are accurately told about the achievements of capitalism operating ethically will be energized and inspired at the prospect of providing excellent services and products for those they serve, enhancing the lives of those they manage, and generating a profit for themselves, their companies, and their fellow citizens. Many of those students will also be galvanized into achieving big things themselves when they are told about the countless inventions, medicines, and other improvements through which capitalist companies have benefited innumerable people. Some of the taken-for granted products that so greatly enhance our lives including—GE and lightbulbs, Carrier and air conditioners, Whirlpool and washers and dryers, Ford and cars, Apple and iPhones, Hewlett Packard and IBM and computers, Kodak and cameras, Otis and elevators, Pfizer and the mass production of antibiotics, represent just a few of the firms that have left their imprint on society due to the pursuit of free-market capitalism. In addition, the whole entertainment industry and most of Silicon Valley enterprises also have grown out of principled capitalism—with the help of venture capitalists, shareholders, and many other stakeholders who have benefitted. Groundbreaking prescription medicines are also usually the result of private enterprise, not, as many people think, developed by the government or at university labs.

Business students should also understand that the free-enterprise system has, by far, generated many more philanthropists than any other economic regime—and that the lives of virtually everyone in our society has been immeasurably enriched by the beneficence of those who share the wealth they have earned. In the United States, everywhere one looks, there are libraries, schools, hospitals, museums, orphanages, homeless shelters, nursing homes, clinics, food kitchens, museums, music and art programs, research centers, scholarships, and foundations of every variety that were either started by or are currently maintained by those who have earned large amounts of money in the free-enterprise system and have generously poured much of their fortunes into organizations that benefit others. For example, Warren Buffett, Bill Gates, and Melinda Gates established The Giving Pledge in 2010 to encourage billionaires around the world to contribute most of their wealth into the society that enabled them to earn it. To date, over 230 of the world's wealthiest people have signed on (givingpledge.org).

In order to energize, encourage, and inspire students by recounting the great achievements principled capitalism has made possible, business administrators and faculty members must be willing to represent this system as it actually is, rather than to vilify it. As Novak (1996) recognizes, although capitalism has its problems, it is by far the best economic system when compared to all others. He writes that:

> Democracy, Winston Churchill once said, is a bad system of government, except when compared to all the others. Much the same might be said of capitalism. It is not a system much celebrated by poets, philosophers, and priests. From time to time, it has seemed romantic to the young, but not very often. Capitalism is a system that commends itself best to the middle-aged, after they have gained some experience of the way history treats the plans of men.

He notes that young people are often suspicious of the system, and today, under the influence of many modern administrators and instructors, students frequently emerge from school with very negative views of the system in which they will seek employment. Clearly, business schools need to explain to students—and model—the way that virtue is linked to principled capitalism. As Novak (1996) makes clear, a properly functioning free-enterprise system actually depends upon widespread virtue—among the employers, the employees, the customers, and other stakeholders. Barnes (2018) also writes in describing virtuous capitalism, that it "is neither wealth accumulation nor conspicuous consumption, but a genuine desire to see the power of free markets used for the purpose of human flourishing." Consequently, business programs should make it *their* business to teach the ethics and virtues without which free enterprise cannot exist. Every business class should include ethical considerations, the opportunity to cultivate moral reasoning, and the chance to apply these principles in cases studies. Representing principled free enterprise as it actually is should be an ethical imperative. It is cruel, unfair, and untrue—a form of professional malpractice—to represent capitalism only as a shameless, ruthless system that preys upon the week, rewards the rapacious, and victimizes the vast majority of people. It is only just to enlighten young people in general and business students in particular as to the remarkable achievements of the principled free-market system has made possible in the United States.

At a time when many young people are eager to achieve social justice in many areas, it is particularly important for them to understand that such advances cannot be made if the economic system does not generate the funds to subsidize them. To that end, business administrators and faculty need to help students realize that there has never, in the history of the world, been a better system for generating fairly earned profit than principled capitalism. As Novak (1996) discussed, capitalism is responsible for lifting untold millions—and whole countries—out of poverty. He recognized that no economic system has done more to alleviate widespread misery. In Novak's (1990) book, *The Spirit of Democratic Capitalism,* he wrote, "Democratic capitalism is neither the Kingdom of God nor without sin. Yet all other known systems of political economy are worse. Such hope as we have for alleviating poverty and for removing oppressive tyranny—perhaps our last, best hope—lies in this much despised system." In 1996, Novak further elaborated that "Many persons educated in the humanities (with their aristocratic traditions) and the social sciences (with their quantifying, collectivist traditions) are uncritically anticapitalist. They think of business as vulgar, philistine, and morally suspect." These are often the people in our academic institutions that shape the philosophy of the students in business departments.

A commitment must be made to repeatedly promote the basic tenets of and positive features of capitalism to business students so that they are proud of their chosen vocations and become committed to using their talents to benefit society in a multitude of ways. Lorenzi (2012) forcefully makes the very obvious, but often unmentioned point that wealth must be created before it can be used to benefit the poor:

> The primary purpose of business schools is to teach wealth creation. Unlike the recent social policy infatuation with debt creation, business schools and business organizations realize the importance of wealth creation. Critics and the media conflate wealth creation with its ignoble side, wealth accumulation. Worse, critics confuse wealth with income, consumption or GDP. Anticapitalism critics of business schools view greed (wealth accumulation) as the primary goal, and capitalism as the primary method to pursue wealth. Proponents of social justice, criticizing business schools and capitalism as the cause of poverty and inequality, ignore the fact that income and wealth need first to be created before it can be re-distributed. Without wealth creation, there is no wealth to share, no justice to be had. And without some

wealth accumulation, there is nothing to invest in the future and no incentive to create wealth.

As Bono, singer and celebrity, so eloquently said at Georgetown's Global Social Enterprise Initiative in 2011, "Entrepreneurial capitalism takes more people out of poverty than aid" (Tanner, 2012). What he failed to mention is that aid is also most readily made available through capitalist systems. Business programs should highlight the remarkable progress that capitalistic societies have made in elevating standards of living and should focus on the trickle-down effects of financial prosperity. There is much data to document the benefits that students should be exposed to. For example:

> Countries in the top quartile of the Cato Institute's annual Economic Freedom of the World Index had an average per capita GDP of $31,501 in 2009, compared with $4,545 for those nations in the bottom quartile. The poorest 10 percent of the population in the most economically free nations had an income more than twice the average income in the least economically free nations. (Tanner, 2012)

Business schools must work to provide a greater focus on the benefits that capitalism can bring, especially if practiced ethically.

Proving the Business Programs' Value to the College

Overall, this chapter has addressed the way that most current business programs fail to operate in a business-like manner and how frequently they fail to operate as though they valued the for-profit motive that is a cornerstone of the free marketplace. Under this heading, we have described some other widespread inadequacies in business programs and have discussed some of the ways that administrators and faculties could update and improve their offerings to make them more attractive to students and more valuable to their students and to their prospective employers. This chapter concludes with some thoughts on one of the other underlying issues that undermines many business programs, as well as the low morale among many administrators, faculty, and students in these programs.

Many outside the academy may be surprised to hear that those in business programs in colleges and universities often are thought of as second- or third-class citizens. Many of the administrators and faculties in the other fields frankly look down on their colleagues in business and have less respect for business students than for those in other disciplines. Consequently, those in business programs constantly need to defend the academic value of business as a discipline. At many institutions, other program areas routinely disparage business schools. Some of the resentment is articulated by Conn, a history professor at Miami University in Ohio, after his department received the business school's used furniture. "The business school growing ever bigger and ever wealthier while humanities departments shrink and suffer and starve, grateful for the leftovers tossed at us by our business-school betters" (Conn, 2018). Perhaps some of the resentment is justified when it is directed at the high proportion of donor money that floods to business schools and is almost nonexistent in the humanities, but there is often disparagement of the business school for not being "scholarly" enough in its teaching. This, despite most courses in the business curriculum being grounded in psychology, sociology, anthropology, and mathematics. Conn (2018) suggests the anti-capitalist leaning that we described above in writing that:

> Many of us in the arts and sciences simply don't believe that teaching business techniques constitutes the real work universities ought to do. We may not quite believe in the disinterested search for truth the way our predecessors once did, but we bristle at the idea that a university ought to promote profit-making as a goal unto itself.

Many in the humanities and the straight sciences consider business to be too unintellectual, often assuming that business faculty and students generally have too little general education in history, philosophy, literature, the arts, philosophy, and theology. Scientists, in evaluating business programs, often think their business colleagues and students have too little proficiency in the hard sciences and research focus. Additionally, the social scientists often think that those in business do not have a "pure" interest in the theoretical aspects of psychology, sociology, political science, and so on, and assume that the business interest in these fields is purely in connection with making money. The professoriat in the humanities, the sciences, and the social sciences all tend to think that those focusing on business are interested in the application of knowledge and in the making of money—both of which the others—theoretically at least—deride. An additional reason for this disdain is that the students with the top-grade point averages and those considered most academically talented are rarely business majors. Although education administrators, faculty, and students are often also looked down upon by the others because they too deal in the application of knowledge and in methods of delivery, the education group frequently devalues business colleagues and students as well. Why? Because the Education faculty and students believe that education is a higher calling than business. Furthermore, since most of those in education typically earn much less than those in business, they believe that they cannot be accused of greed—a trait that they often attribute to those in business.

Some of the ongoing ridicule of the pre-professional areas of the university comes from those who feel that a college degree should involve broad, liberal thinking. Guroian (2002) claims that business education strips undergraduate students of their idealism. Lorenzi (2012) critiques Guroian's contention when he writes that:

> It is the liberal, general education curriculum that is the common experience for students of accredited business schools as well as the first half of the baccalaureate education for most business students. It is not uncommon for business students, schooled first in the liberal arts core, with courses in writing, speaking and critical thinking, to move on to the business school curriculum unable to write, speak or think critically. Liberal arts critics of business school have no training in business, no understanding of statistics, no appreciation of the world of work outside the university.

Clearly, this issue is one that needs to be solved at the college or university level, but business administrators and faculty could help themselves and their students by accurately representing principled free enterprise, by touting its successes, and by demonstrating the tremendous value that well-run businesses generate for our whole society. In other words, many of our business colleagues would do well to teach and encourage Michael Novak's view of "Business as a Calling," based on fundamental virtues, that enables each individual in business to simultaneously work for the common good and to promote his or her own welfare.

Another important way to help remove the academic stigma often attached to business programs is to find thoughtful ways to incorporate the liberal arts into this pre-professional discipline in meaningful ways. If business programs and the practice of business itself were more highly regarded, it would lead to more profitable business programs because more students would flock to them and satisfied parents, employers, and alumni might be more willing to donate funds to support them.

Business programs typically offer a profitable area of the college because of the low overhead they operate under compared to other academic areas. Large number of students can be served in a classroom without any of the lab or specific internship requirements that other pre-professional programs demand. At a time when many colleges are facing financial austerity, profitable areas of the college, such as business, are worth nurturing and developing further. College administrators must be creative in the ways that they tap into the profit potential of the business school. For example, recently at our college, five-year undergraduate/MBA programs were developed for undergraduate English and Math majors. This brings students to the business program with strong communication and quantitative skills and helps these liberal arts students gain access to a competitive job market.

Business schools should require strong prerequisite competencies in the liberal arts so that their students will have more developed skills in logic, reasoning, and communication, as well as more general knowledge. This will make them better students, boost their own self-esteem, and also make them more attractive to employers. Business students also need to be better prepared in some other fields, as well as to incorporate some of the competencies from those areas into their mastery of business. Business training utilizes many of the social sciences, as well as mathematics and engineering. Administrators need to clarify the strong academic bases for success in a business program, and, ideally, need to hire faculty who demonstrate that background themselves. At the collegiate and also programmatic level, administrators and faculty members should recognize that well-educated, thinking businesspeople with a strong background in the liberal arts will benefit themselves, their employers and society at large.

CONCLUSION

Many business programs have been operating at sub-optimum levels for decades, but the recent digital disruption in society, the acceleration of the processes of business itself, and the crises brought on by the pandemic have made improvement more urgent. The financial insolvency of many business programs (and colleges), the fiscal instability and unsustainability of some others, and the failure of most to operate at a profit merely emphasizes that many of our business programs are at a critical juncture and that immediate improvements must be made if many are to survive. According to Sasse (2019):

> Because of the uncertainty over the job futures (job insecurity) of college graduates and income instability and technological uncertainties ahead, we should be asking harder questions of those who would lead our colleges and universities through the digital disruption of society. We should raise big questions about purpose and effectiveness, about technology and place, and about human capital, both inside and outside the school. The time to tolerate complacency has long since passed, and everyone who cares about the future of this critical sector and about helping our students navigate a change that's every bit as big as industrialization and urbanization should be demanding more.

Business programs, and the larger colleges in which they reside, should continually assess their programs—and not simply from an accrediting standpoint. This assessment should include eliminating unproductive programs, strategically modifying those that need to be improved, and introducing innovative courses that keep pace with the changing marketplace and that are responsive to students' and employers' needs. Administrators and faculty should also cultivate the business mindset of successful entrepreneurs who constantly look for ways to gain a competitive advantage, establish new market niches, add value to their products, and take advantage of opportunities that present themselves—or better still, create those opportunities.

For many years, the market supported the uniformity of programs and rapidly increasing prices—funded, in a large part, by growing admissions, student loans, increasing endowments, and other government subsidies. This is no longer the case. In many instances, admissions are falling, the market of traditional students is shrinking, student loans themselves are becoming untenable burdens for a large percentage of young people, and the default ratio on these loans is mushrooming. Under these circumstances, business as usual simply is not an option. Students and parents are at a crossroads. They are seeking greater value in education at lower prices. This is a quintessential business problem (provide a better product at a lower price) that America's collegiate and university business programs must solve if they are to survive.

REFERENCES

Barnes, K. (2018). *Redeeming capitalism.* Eerdmans.

Barrett, B. (2010). Quoted by Tom Tresser: Time for new thinking & being in our business schools. Retrieved November 15, 2011, from https://blog.americansforthearts.org/2019/05/15/time-for-new-thinking-being-in-our-business-schools

Belkin, D. (2022, July 20). Broke colleges resort to mergers for survival. *The Wall Street Journal.*

Bennett W., & Wilezol, D. (2013). *Is college worth it?* Thomas Nelson Publishers.

Bennis W., & O'Toole, J. (2005, May). How business schools lost their way. *Harvard Business Review.*

Conn, S. (2018, February 20). Business schools have no business in the university. *The Chronicle of Higher Education.* https://www.chronicle.com/article/business-schools-have-no-business-in-the-university/

Datar, S., Garvin, D., & Cullen, P. (2010). Rethinking the M.B.A.: Business education at a crossroads. *Harvard Business Review Press.* https://www.hbs.edu/faculty/Pages/item.aspx?num=37295

De-Costa-Klipa, N. (2019, March 25). *The 'perfect storm' behind the recent college closings and how it could change New England.* Boston.com. https://www.boston.com/news/schools/2019/03/25/college-closings-in-new-england/

Denning, S. (2018, May 27). Why today's business schools teach yesterday's expertise. *Forbes.*

Jacobs, M. (2009, April 24). How business schools have failed business. *The Wall Street Journal.*

Friga, P., Bettis, R., & Sullivan, R. (2003). Changes in graduate management education and new business school strategies for the 21st century. *Academy of Management Learning and Education Journal, 2*(2), 233–249.

The Giving Pledge. (2010). https://givingpledge.org/

Guroian, V. (2002). Why should businessmen read great literature. *Religion and Liberty.*

Hess, F., & Addison, G. (2018, August 29). *Apple, Google, et al. strike a blow against the college cartel.* National Review.com. https://www.nationalreview.com/2018/08/employers-stop-requiring-college-degrees-that-arent-needed/

Lorenzi, P. Business Schools: Capitalism's Last Stand. Soc 49, 230–239 (2012). https://doi.org/10.1007/s12115-012-9536-x

Lapovsky, L. (2018, February 6). The changing business model for colleges and universities. *Forbes.*

Metropolitan State University of Denver. (n.d.). https://www.msudenver.edu/hospitality/our-story/hospitality-learning-center/

Mintzberg, H. (2005). *Managers Not MBAs: A hard look at the soft practice of managing and management development paperback.* Berrett-Koehler.

Novak, M. (1990). *The spirit of democratic capitalism.* Templeton Press.

Novak, M. (1996). *Business as a calling.* The Free Press.

Rao, D. (2015, May 2). Should business school deans know real business? *Forbes.*

Reynolds, G. (2012). *The higher education bubble.* Encounter Books.

Sasse, B. (2019, September 4). 17 questions every college should be asking. *The Atlantic.* https://www.theatlantic.com/ideas/archive/2019/09/17-questions-every-college-should-be-asking/597310/

Sheeran, J. (2000). Anticapitalism at business school. *The Free Market.* https://mises.org/library/anticapitalism-business-school

Tanner, M. (2012). *Capitalism's triumph.* http://www.nationalreview.com/article/358771/capitalisms-triumph-michael-tanner

University of People. (2023). *58 weird college majors not to be missed.* uopeople.edu. https://www.uopeople.edu/blog/weird-college-majors/

U.S. News & World Report. (2023). *2022–2023 College Rankings.* https://www.usnews.com/best-colleges/rankings/internship-programs

Worthen, M. (2022). This is not your grandfather's M.B.A. *The New York Times.* https://www.nytimes.com/2022/05/05/opinion/business-schools-capitalism-mba.html

Yonk, R., & Simmons, R. (2017). *Reinventing how business schools teach morality of capitalism, business ethics and entrepreneurship.* John Templeton Foundation.

CHAPTER 4

THE SCHISM BETWEEN THE SCHOLARLY AND THE APPLIED

ABSTRACT

This chapter discusses the diminishing value of a business degree, sometimes resulting from the failure of educational institutions to adequately prepare students for the needs of the workplace. Several suggestions are offered that can help to better prepare students with the competencies that will be needed in a new economy. These are largely related to the relationships between academic institutions and the external business world.

Keywords: business school curricula, stakeholders, differentiation, employer competencies, strategic alliances

INTRODUCTION

In the following chapter, we discuss what we feel is one of the most serious problems facing business schools and those factors that are contributing to the diminishing value of a business degree. The chapter will discuss the academic research problem within business schools and the barriers to the dissemination of organizational research. It will also discuss the new competencies that are sought in employees and that are often being overlooked by academics. Largely to blame for the widening divide between what is taught in business schools and what can be applied in the contemporary business workplace are those administrative failures that we highlighted in Chapters 2 and 3. Some potential administrative solutions are provided to address the problems creating these deficiencies. In Chapter 5, we elaborate on the ways that service-learning can be instituted as a pedagogical tool for minimizing this divide.

A How-To Guide for Business School Practitioners, pp. 49–63

A major challenge to business schools, as we outlined in the earlier chapters, is to become more relevant to stakeholders. One of the greatest problems in the realm of business education is the researching and teaching of material that is often inconsequential in a new economy. Organizational theories are thought to describe organizational phenomena in ways that can help managers to improve productivity and, in turn, the human condition. In the classroom, however, the academic research that is relied upon by instructors is often disconnected from "real-world" occurrences. In the workplace too, managers most often have no exposure to the academic theories that are supposed to provide guidance to them. If theories do reach practitioners and have any type of relevancy, it is often not until a time when operational contexts have substantially shifted, thus weakening theory applicability and potential. The limitations on knowledge diffusion are disturbing when students and businesses could potentially benefit from much of the ongoing research that is generated in academia (von Feigenblatt, 2013).

McCauley et al. (2007) noted the irony in that much management-orientated theory and research is not read by managers. These authors claim that part of this problem has to do with a tendency on the part of researchers to focus on restricted theoretical preoccupations. As McCauley et al. further note:

> Although these narrow concerns are easier to research and meet the dominant standards of methodological rigour they often result in apparently trivial findings from the point of view of practising managers. Moreover, the findings are usually only published in peer reviewed academic journals that are unread by practising managers. (p. 21)

The publish or perish cultures that have arisen at most academic institutions have allowed for this specialized, sometimes useless work to proliferate. Some academics—veiling their single-topic, recurring research streams as in-depth analyzes—have created the narrow focus that is deemed irrelevant by practitioners, and which fails to prepare students for their future work. College business programs, which should be the source of ideas and solutions for businesses, are rarely used by the business community because of this focus that is viewed as being unrelated to real-world matters.

Institutionalization

The re-creation of practices such as those related to publish or perish is rampant in academia and has led to the proliferation of business programs across the nation that are very similar to each other, and which have the same weaknesses. Although successful business leaders strive to differentiate their products and services in order to achieve better returns than their competitors, there is a persistent lack of differentiation between colleges and universities that can largely be attributed to institutionalism. Institutionalism occurs when organizations actively copy one another's practices, and results in substantial isomorphism. According to organizational research, meaning is socially constructed among large numbers of organizations through the creation of shared practices and the collective attribution of rationality or justice to those practices (DiMaggio & Powell, 1991, 1983; Meyer & Rowan, 1977; Scott, 1995). Institutional forces are quite apparent in college business programs for these reasons; most tend to resemble each other due to the adaptation of similar practices. Dimaggio and Powell (1983) further described this isomorphism as "the constraining process that forces one unit in a population to resemble other units that face the same set of environmental conditions." This similarity may help institutions to deal with environmental uncertainty but also leads to a homogeneity across organizations that can stifle innovation and prosperity. The lack of differentiation, coupled with the sharp rise in prices, has spurred traditional college students and their families to explore new educational alternatives which include online programs, vocational programs, company-provided training and community colleges.

Some of the factors that contribute to isomorphism include the cultural expectations held by society, governmental and accrediting body mandates, and imitation brought on by uncertainty and diffused through employee migration or hired consulting firms. Also at work, according to the institutional isomorphism theories, are normative pressures that are brought about from the profession itself.

> One mode is the legitimization inherent in the licensing and crediting of educational achievement. The other is the inter-organizational networks that span organizations. Norms developed during education are entered into organizations. Inter-hiring between existing industrial firms also encourages isomorphism. People from the same educational backgrounds will approach problems in much the same way. Socialization on the job reinforces these conformities. (Dimaggio & Powell, 1983)

In academia, we witness a lack of diversity in political and social ideology among professors. This can be attributed to institutional forces that require schools to hire graduates from similar accredited institutions. The research universities, where much doctoral training occurs, are often homogenous in their programs and teachings, and the process serves to recreate indistinguishable organizations.

The lack of diversity within college business programs can also be linked to a lack of creativity among business professionals in the field. Cohan wrote in *Forbes* in 2014 that, "[i]t's been about 20 years since a powerful idea came along that galvanized executives to invest in changing their business." He posits that the dearth of idea generation can be attributed to a "lack of clever idea generators" and highlights that this is the case even though "there are many business books that get published every year—very few of which get any traction—and tens of thousands of young people study business in colleges and MBA programs around the world."

We suspect that the shortage of inspiring ideas can be partially attributed to the lack of diversity among business professors and, in turn, their students. When we speak of diversity, we are referring to the diversity of mindsets, values, and philosophies. Because so many academics have been trained at similar accredited schools of business by instructors who have shared the same academic heritages, variation in the types of ideas that these people are capable of producing may be constrained. This homogenous thinking has contributed to the lack of strategic growth at many business schools (Tolan, 2015).

Accrediting Organizations

Frequently, within ads for tenure track business faculty, we see the Qualifications requiring a PhD from an AACSB (The Association to Advance Collegiate Schools of Business) accredited program. This sort of restrictive selection process works to diminish the diversity of ideas that will be shared and the encounters that students and faculty members will experience. Widespread practices like this—even though they are purported to strengthen standards—also limit the breadth of faculty members. The advancement of a business program and its relationship with the external business community can be inhibited by the accrediting body's reach into hiring decisions in this way.

The homogenous environments that institutionalism has created have led to the similar requirements for faculty tenure and promotion that were discussed in Chapter 1. We highlighted the converging requirements for faculty, regardless of the type of college that they are affiliated with. These requirements have contributed to a system in which business schools are inadequately preparing future leaders (Holstein, 2013).

The Scientific Method and Promotion and Tenure Requirements

Within the business school, some of the most noticeable isomorphic effects can be witnessed in the types of research that are conducted and the types of publications that "count" as acceptable to promotion and tenure committees. Bennis and O'Toole (2005), in their comprehensive discussion of the failings of the modern business school, suggest that the unproductive system began its slide in 1959 when both the Ford and Carnegie Foundations criticized business education for its unscientific foundation. As they recount:

> The result? Half a century of business school research that aspired to be "scientific." The problem is that in a field of human activity that is undergoing dramatic change, findings that can be proven to be universally true by double-blind scientific experiments turn out to be of little practical utility. Research therefore came to be evaluated on the elegance and rigor of the experimental design more than on the utility of the findings. The fact that few, if any, business people ever tried to read, let alone implement, the research was considered irrelevant. Business school research is an enclosed self-referential world—academics writing for other academics. The utility of the entire research enterprise is not a fit subject for discussion.

Bennis and O'Toole (2005) further contend that scientific research is appropriate as Aristotle envisioned it, in a world that *cannot be other than it is*. It is not, however, fully applicable to a world where things can be much different than they appear—or "other than they appear." This is the case in the business world in which explanations for business phenomena can be sought in the social sciences such as psychology, social psychology, sociology, anthropology and political science. These academic areas can often be utilized to provide insight regarding business events, and their very humanistic nature prohibits a reliance on a purely scientific model. Bennis and O'Toole also note that:

> That part of the world consists of people—of relationships, of interactions, of exchanges. In this part of the world, relationships can be good, bad or indifferent; close, distant or sporadic. They change—they can be other than they currently are. For this part of the world, Aristotle said that the method used to develop our understanding and to shape this world is rhetoric; dialogue between parties that builds understanding that actually shapes and alters this part of the world. (Bennis & O'Toole, 2005)

Because of the models and systems that have been so thoroughly ingrained into business schools, "genuine reform of the MBA curriculum remains elusive. This is probably because the curriculum is the effect, not the cause, of what ails the modern business school" (McNamara, 2006). McNamara (2006) continues that:

> The actual cause of today's crisis in management education is far broader in scope than most of us want to believe, and it can be traced to a dramatic

shift in the culture of business schools. During the past several decades, many leading business schools have quietly adopted an inappropriate and ultimately self-defeating-model of academic excellence. Instead of measuring themselves in terms of the competence of their graduates, or by how well their faculties understand important drivers of business performance, schools measure themselves almost solely by the rigor of their scientific research. They have adopted a model of science that uses abstract financial and economic analysis, statistical multiple regressions, and laboratory psychology. Much of this research is excellent, but because so little of it is grounded in actual *business* practices, the focus of graduate business education has become increasingly circumscribed—and increasingly less relevant to practitioners.

Denning (2018) goes as far as to say that "what is taught by a business school hardly matters. That's because business schools mainly perform a "filtering' function ('selection of the sharpest analytic minds') rather than a teaching function ('what is good management practice for a 21st century firm?')." An MBA is now "a highly valued credential, but you're not going to learn much along the way" (Denning, 2018). The weaknesses in the business school model, however, have not been prominently exposed to prospective students until recently. A system that was designed to train managers in radically different times is proving to be deficient for preparing today's business students. Businesses rarely rely upon academia to provide the solutions to management problems that they seek (Denning, 2018; Khurana, as cited in Holstein, 2013). Management consulting firms are employed instead, typically at a high cost to the business firm. Interestingly:

> McKinsey [a top management consulting firm] sends many of its non-MBAs to a 3–4 week mini-MBA boot camp to learn the most important tools and concepts. In 1993, 61% of new McKinsey recruits had MBAs, but that number is now down to less than half, which demonstrates that McKinsey believes it quickly trains non-MBAs to be consultants. (ManagementConsultEd, 2021)

The McKinsey practice appears to be in line with other major U.S employers who are seeking employees who possess the aptitude to learn, to be team players and to merge well into distinctive organizational cultures.

This failure of business schools to effectively prepare students for work in the modern economy needs to be addressed by academic administrators if these schools are to regain their standing. They were once thought of as the best ways to prepare for careers in the upper echelons of corporate America but are now more frequently criticized for what amounts to malpractice.

New Competencies Sought

The denigration of business schools is becoming more pronounced with the public acknowledgement of a student loan crisis. Diverse stakeholder groups have begun to criticize a system that often fails to prepare students for success in a rapidly changing workplace. Some of the differences between the competencies that have been addressed at business schools for many years and those that are required for success in this new era are contrasted later in this chapter. There are many difficulties associated with changing business school models and, as Denning (2018) notes:

> Despite individual thought-leaders in business schools, there has been little change in the core curricula of business school teaching as a whole. The disconnect between what is taught and the vast ongoing societal drama under way continues. And it's difficult to discuss, because it puts in question careers, competencies, job tenure, values, goals, assumptions of the entire business-school world and more. (Denning, 2018)

Management must be conducted in a different manner from what was effective and led to success in the 20th century. Business schools must attempt to address the new competencies in their curricula, but some of these are quite difficult to teach. Denning (2018) notes that the successful firms that we witness in this new economy have exercised the following practices:

- Managers can't tell people what to do;
- Control is enhanced by letting go of control;
- Talent drives strategy;
- Dealing with big issues requires small teams, small tasks, small everything;
- Complex systems are inherently problematic, and must be descaled;
- Companies make more money by not focusing on money. (Denning, 2018)

As Denning (2018) highlights, the conditions for business success have radically been altered in recent years as we have entered a 4th Industrial Revolution (Industry 4.0). The new industrial landscape is characterized by :

> the ongoing automation of traditional manufacturing and industrial practices, using modern smart technology. Large-scale machine-to-machine communication (M2M) and the internet of things (IoT) are integrated for

increased automation, improved communication and self-monitoring, and production of smart machines that can analyze and diagnose issues without the need for human intervention. (Moore, 2020)

Business schools should, accordingly, change the preparation they provide. This will involve new teaching methods regarding management, leadership, group behavior, financial analysis, and problem solving, to note a few.

We discuss below some of the competencies that employers are demanding in this 4th Industrial Society as contrasted to those that were necessary in earlier the 3rd Industrial Society—the fourth which is characterized by the adoption of digital computing and communications technology ("Digital Revolution, 2021). The managers in the 3rd Industrial Society were still largely working in centralized positions, with strict procedures and rules regarding how to perform. The 4th Industrial Age—in contrast to the third—allows workers the ability to use technology on their own and supports work from remote locations and flexible systems of work. In the United States- where the economy is heavily focused upon innovation as opposed to manufacturing- new competencies are necessary in order to be successful (see Table 4.1).

Table 4.1

Competencies Sought: Old Versus New

Competencies for Old Economy	Competencies for New Economy
Specialist	Generalist
Analytical	Analytical and Communicative
Information Seeker	Information Critic
Use of Efficient Procedures to Motivate	Appropriate Use of Artificial Intelligence
Knowledge of National Distinctive Cultures	Global Mind Set

Employers need workers who can innovate in a fast-moving environment. Globalization precipitated the need for companies to become leaner and more flexible. This has diminished bureaucratic controls and the specialization that they supported. Graduates who can think creatively and who can respond to understand the needs of colleagues from multiple functional areas of the firm are now in great demand.

Instead of a broad distinction between those in the "hard skills" functions (such as finance, engineering and accounting professionals) and those involved with "soft skills" (such as human resource, marketing and management professionals), there is now a need for employees who are strong in both. In accounting, for example, as is highlighted in Chapter 6, we have seen a movement toward the strengthening of communication and critical thinking skills in the undergraduate curriculum. The CPA examination has been adjusted so that problems are addressed both quantitatively and qualitatively. Similarly, the demand for effective communicators is competitive in all fields. All employees who expect to advance in a business firm should be able to work analytically in their own technical area but should also be able to effectively work with others and to clearly communicate what they are doing, why they are doing it, and how it relates to the strategic focus of the firm.

We now have access to more information than we can effectively sort and process. The information age that we are living in has created its own problems in that we have an overabundance of information, which we must filter and make sense of. This 4th Industrial Revolution—as it is referred to- and the accompanying need for continuous innovation—will require teaching that hones holistic decision-making skills, flexibility, strong quantitative analysis and clear, appropriate communications. Denning (2018) discusses training and technology in this new economy:

> Let's be clear: the differences between leaders and losers isn't a matter of access to *technology*, or *big data* or *artificial intelligence*. Both the successful and unsuccessful firms have access to the same technology, data and AI, which are now largely commodities. Traditionally-managed firms use the same technology and data but typically get meager results. It's not technology or data or AI that make the difference. The difference lies in the nimbler way these firms deploy technology, data and AI. Until recently, the lack of familiarity in business schools with the new way of running organizations could in part be excused because the management expertise itself was still somewhat obscure. There was little awareness of it outside software development, and general management thinkers had little respect for management ideas coming from software developers. That's no longer the case. (Denning, 2018)

Contemporary managers need training that is quite different from that which effectively prepared managers for work in the 3rd Industrial society, one in which management was top-down, where workers focused mainly in their functional roles, and where technology was used to network and assist rather than take on primary business functions.

PROPOSED SOLUTIONS

Professional Models Instead of Scientific Models

We increasingly hear the recommendation that business schools should follow "the professional model" of medical and law schools instead of the "scientific model" of graduate schools of arts and science (Bennis &

O'Toole, 2005; McNamara, 2006). McNamara (2006) notes, "The professional model combines practice and theory and presumes that most or all teachers will have some practical experience." The earlier discussion of the evolving current model highlights the lack of utility that academic research from business schools has on the external business world. Movement to a new type of model will require dedication and creativity on the part of academic practitioners.

Complicating the job that business school deans will face in moving from the scientific model is the dilemma caused by the numerical ratings provided annually to selected programs (DeAngelo et al., 2005). These serve to stifle program development as schools often seek to improve rankings by employing short-term strategies instead of investing in knowledge creation. Instead of "practicing what they preach" about the dangers of short-term thinking and the importance of substance over form in business practices, administrators put effort into those factors that are weighted most heavily by the raters, including starting salaries and return on tuition investment.

> Rankings mania also leads business schools to distort MBA curricula with "quick fix, look good" changes that enhance program marketability at the expense of providing students with a rigorous, conceptual education that will serve them well over their entire careers. (DeAngelo et al., 2005)

These ratings are also not reflective of students' character and values that may have developed over time in a business program.

Increased Association Between Practitioners and Academics

In an effort to narrow the divide between academia and the business world, academics need to work to form alliances between their schools and external business firms. As the focus of business schools has moved toward research and away from "real-world" applications, their reputations have suffered along with enrollments. In Chapter 5, we discuss several ways that service-learning can be used in business programs to help them to fulfill their missions while involving business students in projects that will allow them to experience business world problems and issues while still in school. These projects appear to enhance student empathy (Astin & Sax, 1998) and student dispositions towards future performance of organizational citizenship behaviors (Tolan, 2007). At a time when the scientific model at business schools is under scrutiny and emotional intelligence and well-honed communication skills are sought from employees, service-learning projects represent tools that have great potential for the business schools that engage in them.

Workforce Training

Workforce training represents a potential revenue stream for college business programs that is largely underutilized because of the perceived lack of relevance of academic material to businesses. Relationships between individual companies and colleges can be formed for delivery of degree programs or to provide ongoing training to employees that will keep their skills relevant.

In a widely publicized alliance, Starbucks and Arizona State University have established what they call the Starbucks College Achievement Plan under which any employee who works at least 20 hours per week can complete their junior and senior years of college online at the university. Students are expected to work their 20+ hours while becoming full-time students. In this creative venture, a business model is applied.

> Although ASU is a public university, its online wing is definitely a revenue-generating enterprise, helping the university manage its finances in an era of declining state aid. Online courses are taught by ASU professors, but much of the technical and administrative work that goes into managing ASU Online has been handed over to a private company, Pearson. (Reznikoff, 2014)

In 2019, after 5 years of this collaborative program, over 3000 Starbucks employees had graduated from ASU (ASU News, 2019).

These types of strategic alliances do not have to be administered at the scale of a large institution like ASU and countless opportunities exist among firms in the areas surrounding most academic institutions if college administrators are creative and business oriented in their execution. Colleges must give employers what they demand, and what better way to do this than to form strategic alliances and to collaborate for mutually beneficial programs.

Employ More Practitioners

The lack of perceived relevance between the research conducted and taught by career academics and the training that employers demand presents a major hurdle to business school administrators. As Drobny (2005) notes in response to Heskitt's (2005) article, *How Can Business Schools Be Made More Relevant?*, "If the institution places research-focused faculty or graduate students in front of students, and the students lack any perspective gained through experience, the outcome will do little to enhance the managerial skill sets of the graduates." The tendency in academia has been to hire full-time faculty who have limited business experience and a terminal degree in the field in which they are to specialize and teach. Adjunct instructors who are practitioners in the business world have then been hired to bring hands-on knowledge to the students. The commitment that a full-time employee brings to the institution and, in this case, to the students, is weakened through this model. Leonard Land (as cited in McNamara, 2006) agrees that "Relevancy requires that the MBA-level instructor be a true practitioner-scholar who has ... run or been a key part of a global business and has an advanced degree." If colleges are to shift to a more professional model for their business programs, they will have to recognize the important role that experienced practitioners should play in training students for the workplace. The tenure track model that currently dominates academic business programs might have to be supplemented by professional tracks that hire and promote those with business experience who prove to be effective teachers and who commit themselves well to college affairs.

Teacher Training

We have witnessed academic colleagues who are adamant about never referring to a professor as a teacher. Their logic is that professors operate at a level far above the practical level and should be able to convey concepts to students that might be translated into practical use by students at a later date. Despite these good intentions, it appears that much of what is presented at the abstract level fails to create utility in the form of work skills. Many business professors begin their careers in academia without proper consideration of what good teaching in the discipline should encompass. There are often no training programs for those with doctorates prior to teaching business courses at the college or master's level. Lisa Marks Dolan, a business school dean, "feels that much of the problem lies in the way teachers are trained: We're being asked to produce graduates who can integrate, adapt, manage global diversity, work in teams, and bring out the best in others, yet these are not the skills that most doctoral candidates are asked to master as part of their training" (as cited in McNamara, 2006).

Strategic Dissemination of Work

It appears obvious that those responsible for developing theories in the area of business management need to develop and disseminate their work strategically so that the work can become meaningful to practitioners. Unfortunately, this is rarely the case. As Price (2011) writes, "the lack of connection between the theoretical and practical worlds undermines the quality of both disciplines and results in unnecessary hardship by practitioners and inadequately informed efforts by theorists." In Chapter 1 of this book, we have discussed the ways in which colleges and universities are challenged today to make themselves more relevant to their customers and the wider society. Making academic research more useful to business practitioners and engaging business programs in alliances with businesses can create competitive advantages. Academics need to write about issues that are pertinent to contemporary business people and need to work to present their work to business leaders. There are many small, local businesses that would welcome input from academic experts about how to proceed in business operations, but these groups are often overlooked by academics who look for flashy publications.

Novel Programming

As we continually emphasize, college business administrators will have to break from tradition in novel ways if they are to develop innovative, profitable programs. An example of creative programming is flexible, online programs that can be improved upon in order to accommodate a broader population of students. For example, Thomas (2020), recommends that "students could spend several years on their MBAs and then have opportunities to 'top-up' their skills over their lifetimes, either as part of an alumni benefit or as a Netflix-style subscription service."

Some colleges have begun to offer certificate programs that emphasize the development of specific business skills or prepare students for professional certifications. These can offer a profitable way to deploy resources that the business program already possesses. Thirty-nine percent of business schools that are accredited by the AACSB reported offering graduate-level certificates in 2021. Harvard Business School Online now offers certificates instead of degrees. This program started more than 6 years ago with 500 students and now has 30,000. These types of programming offer good solutions for people who need to stay working and who are looking for cost efficiency in the specific programs that they choose. The student loan crisis has highlighted the debt burden that many graduates bear and has led many business program prospects to reconsider enrolling in costly degree programs.

CONCLUSION

The changes to business schools that are necessary for their survival will be very difficult to implement. Hiring those who are like-minded and with similar training exists in both the business school and in the corporation, and these inert forces present formidable challenges.

Norms regarding the hiring of practitioners as instructors will have to be reconsidered if students are to be trained to meet the needs of the contemporary organization. The current tenure process may have to be modified at the business school level in order for this to occur.

The following chapter elaborates on service-learning in depth as it presents a strong opportunity for academic work to be applied—benefiting students, colleges, and the organizations that are served.

REFERENCES

Astin, A. W., & Sax, L. J. (1998). How undergraduates are affected by service participation. *Journal of College Student Development, 39*(3), 251–263.

ASU News. (2019). Retrieved February 5, 2021, from http://news.asu.edu/20191015-sun-devil-life-five-years-later-starbucks-asu-online-support-flexibility

Bennis, W., & O'Toole, J. (2005, May). How business schools lost their way. *Harvard Business Review.* https://hbr.org/2005/05/how-business-schools-lost-their-way

Cohan, P. (2014, January 6). The death of business ideas. *Forbes.*

DeAngelo, H., DeAngelo, L., & Zimmerman, J. L. (2005, July). *What's really wrong with u.s. business schools?* Available at SSRN: https://ssrn.com/abstract=766404 or http://dx.doi.org/10.2139/ssrn.766404

Denning, S. (2018, May 27). Why today's business schools teach yesterday's expertise. *Forbes.* https://www.forbes.com/sites/stevedenning/2018/05/27/why-todays-business-schools-teach-yesterdays-expertise/?sh=74470267488b

Digital Revolution (2021, February 7). In *Wikipedia.* https://en.wikipedia.org/wiki/Digital_Revolution.

DiMaggio, P. J., & Powell, W. W. (1983). The iron cage revisited: Institutional isomorphism and collective rationality in organizational fields. *American Sociological Review, 48*(1), 45–57.

DiMaggio, P. J., & Powell, W. W. (Eds.). (1991). Introduction. In *The new institutionalism in organizational analysis* (pp. 1–40). University of Chicago Press.

Heskitt, J. (2005, July 4). *How can business schools be made more relevant. Harvard Business School.* https://hbswk.hbs.edu/item/how-can-business-schools-be-made-more-relevant

Holstein, W. (2013). The multipolar MBA. *Strategy+Business.* https://www.strategy-business.com/article/00164

ManagementConsultEd.com. (2021). *Why harvard business school does NOT equal McKinsey.* https://managementconsulted.com/mba-business-school-management-and-strategy-consulting/

McCauley, J., Duberley, J., & Johnson, P., (2007). *Organization theory challenges and perspectives.* Pearson Education Limited.

McNamara, D. (2006, November). The relevance of business school education. What do you think? *Journal of College Teaching and Learning, 3*(11). file:///C:/Users/Ben/Dropbox/PC/Downloads/ciadmin,+Journal+manager,+1654-6556-1-CE.pdf

Meyer, J. W., & Rowan, B. (1977). Institutionalized environments: Formal structure as myth and ceremony. *American Journal of Sociology, 83,* 340 –363.

Moore, M. (2019). What is Industry 4.0? Everything you need to know. *TechRadar.* https://www.techradar.com/news/what-is-industry-40-everything-you-need-to-know

Price, J. (2011). Unifying leadership: Bridging the theory and practice divide. *Journal of Strategic Leadership, 3*(2). https://www.regent.edu/acad/global/publications/jsl/vol3iss2/JSL_V3Is2_Price_pp13- 22.pdf

Reznikoff, N. (2014). Starbucks free tuition plan comes at a cost. *MSNBC.* Retrieved February 5, 2021, from https://www.msnbc.com/msnbc/starbucks-offers-employees-free-tuition-arizona-state-university-online-msna350556

Scott, W. R. (1995). *Institutions and organizations.* SAGE.

Thomas, P. (2020, November 7). The new MBA: Flexible, cheaper and lifelong. *The Wall Street Journal.* https://www.wsj.com/articles/the-new-m-b-a-flexible-cheaper-and-lifelong-11604761238

Tolan, M. (2007). *The relationship between student service-learning and participation in organizational citizenship behaviors.* ProQuest Dissertations. https://www.proquest.com/docview/195183025?sourcetype=Scholarly%20Journals

Tolan, M. (2015). *Institutionalization and the death of ideas in management.* Northeast Business and Economics Association (NBEA) Conference Proceedings. Print ISSN: 1936-2048.

Von Feigenblatt, O. F. (2013). *Integrating theory and practice in business education.* https://doi.org/ 10.2139/ssrn.2595296

CHAPTER 5

BRIDGING THE DIVIDE

"Real-World" Education Through Service-Learning and Experiential Education

ABSTRACT

Service-learning, a form of experiential education, infuses experience into the learning environment and provides the needed bridge to connect classroom theory with real-world business applications. At its core, service-learning is about creating opportunities for students to apply the theory they learn in the classroom to real-world problems and real-world needs (O'Neill, 1990). Service-learning affords students structured opportunities that are intentionally designed to pair their classroom learning with practical business applications that address human and community needs (Jacoby, 1996). Through service-learning, students also engage in a cycle of service and reflection. Tolan (2007) linked participation in service-learning projects with a predisposition to engage in future organizational citizenship behaviors, which can be key drivers of productivity.

Some of the material in this chapter is adopted from Tolan's (2007) doctoral dissertation, which discussed the many benefits of service-learning, specifically, the bearing it could have on preparing students to prepare in the workplace through participation in organizational citizenship behaviors. Since the time the dissertation was published, management theorists have focused a lot of attention on the often undervalued impact of employee participation in these prosocial activities that can have widespread influence on positive organizational functioning.

A How-To Guide for Business School Practitioners, pp. 65–79
Copyright © 2024 by Information Age Publishing
www.infoagepub.com
All rights of reproduction in any form reserved.

Figure 5.1

Critiques of Management Education

In their book, *Management Education and Development: Drift or Thrust Into the 21st Century,* Porter and McKibbin (1988) provide a comprehensive critique of American business schools that is still widely cited. A critical observation that they convey is that business education requires breadth, interaction, and engagement with the external environment. The students that Porter and McKibbin studied may have understood the concepts that they had been taught, but most had little or no opportunity in the educational experience to apply newly acquired knowledge and skills to a real-work setting (Madsen, 2004). Further, Stoll (2020) quotes Tim Sands, President of Virginia Tech, as stating that 'student experience with real-world corporate problems would become table stakes in the job market in years to come. Students really need to be embedded within a workplace that experiences real-life problems, and to look at how organizational leaders resolve those problems. Service-learning provides an avenue for students to bridge the gap that exists between academic studies and real-world activities.

In addition to providing much-needed experience, empirical studies of service-learning and other service activities show that for the experience to have a developmental impact, a reflective component must be present in which participants think about the meaning of their service experiences and connect it with broader social issues and personal values (Eyler & Giles, 1999). Thus, students can be requested to document and discuss what they learned from their service-learning assignments and tasks. This reflective component can also help business students to develop ethical thinking such as that which is discussed in Chapter 8.

Pedagogy and Criteria for Service-Learning

Overall, service-learning can be viewed as a pedagogical tool that can be used to address student ethical development, communication abilities, and decision-making acumen in a hands-on fashion; it may also assist students in succeeding in business and contributing to the larger society. The National and Community Service Act of 1990 defined four specific criteria for service-learning:

1. Students learn and develop through active participation in thoughtfully organized service experiences that meet actual community needs and are coordinated in collaboration with the school and community;

2. The experience is integrated into the student's academic curriculum or provides structured time for a student to think, talk, or write about what the student did and saw during the actual service activity;

3. The experience provides students with opportunities to use newly acquired skills and knowledge in real-life situations in their own communities; and

4. The experience enhances what is taught in school by extending student learning beyond the classroom and into the community and helps to foster the development of a sense of a caring for others. (as cited in Weber and Sleeper, 2002, p. 418)

Generally, for a service-learning project, students are paired with businesses or organizations that have specific needs related to the curriculum of a particular course. Students then perform the needed community service by using course content, allowing them to reflect on their experiences for enhanced learning (Madsen, 2004).

Thus, service-learning should not be viewed simply as student volunteerism. A critical distinction between service-learning and volunteerism is the reciprocal benefit of service-learning; both the served and the server teach one another and grow in the relationship (DiPadova, 2000). The student is serving in order to learn, and those who accept the service are doing so in order to teach the student and benefit their organizations (Stanton, 1994). Service-learning projects should be grounded in academic theory with clear learning objectives. Activities should be constructed to align with these objectives, and reflective components should be clear.

Many opportunities exist for incorporating service-learning into business curricula. The experiences can be tailored to the students' needs and abilities and creativity on the part of instructors and administrators can ensure that these projects are met with enthusiasm on the part of the client organization and the student participants.

For instance, an example of a service-learning project for a marketing management class may include having students produce marketing plans for a local company or not-for-profit. Since course activities are linked to student knowledge of the organization and its management and marketing practices, students should be required to expose themselves to the organization in multiple ways.

Students should also be encouraged to reflect upon and discuss any ethical concerns that may have come to their attention, which provides an avenue for ethical development. For a final project, students could be asked to create a comprehensive marketing plan that discusses the organization's essential strategies and suggestions for it to thrive in the future. Students might also be required to discuss any ethical considerations that their suggested strategies might face. The service-learning experiences can be tailored to the student's abilities and to the types of material that is being focused on. For some examples of business-trelated e-Service-Learning Projects by Degree Level, which Germain (2019) suggests, are included in Appendix A. These suggested projects are suitable for in-classroom courses as well.

Some instructors express hesitancy to engage with service-learning projects for fear that the content of their discipline might be diluted. However, even in disciplines where service-learning opportunities may be limited in early coursework, service-learning can provide an excellent means for students to apply academic material before they enter the workforce. For example, with regard to service-learning opportunities for accounting students, the Internal Revenue Service's Volunteer Income Tax Assistance (VITA; IRS.gov, 2023) Program provides a valuable service-learning opportunity that benefits members of the students' communities. With the VITA collaboration, accounting students who have studied taxation in the classroom receive training from the Internal Revenue Service to prepare tax returns using tax software provided by the IRS. Under the supervision of local IRS agents, students learn how to apply their tax theory by preparing returns for actual clients in their communities who are in need of assistance.

Incorporating service-learning into the business school curriculum takes creativity and careful planning and, because of this, instructors must be committed to working differently than they do with traditional pedagogies. For example, instructors must seek out appropriate organizations for service-learning collaborations and maintain relationships with representatives of the organization while the project is underway. Students who are accustomed to a "passive education," or being fed information and then reverberating it, may sometimes resist the highly active and involved nature of a service-learning project. Thus, these projects may take students out of their comfort zones, much like novel problems that are faced by business leaders.

Eyler and Giles (1999), in what appears to be the most comprehensive study of service-learning to date, found that the opportunity to interact with people from diverse backgrounds in a meaningful way was among the most frequently reported benefits of service-learning. Their study, which involved surveying 1,500 college students at 20 institutions and extensively interviewing 66 students from seven institutions, also revealed that student participation in service-learning projects resulted in the following: reduced stereotyping and greater tolerance for diversity, increased personal development, increased interpersonal development and communication, increased understanding of course material and application of knowledge, increased engagement with and curiosity about course material, stronger reflective practice, increased critical thinking and problem-solving skills, and perspective transformation.

Further, in their study, students reported that helping others through service-learning collaborations contributed to greater self-knowledge, spiritual growth, and personal satisfaction. Thus, service-learning was a predictor of an increased sense of personal efficacy, an increased desire to include service to others in one's career plans, and an increased belief in the usefulness of service-learning in developing career skills over the course of a semester.

Throughout an earlier comprehensive study of service-learning results, Astin and Sax (1998) came to many of the same conclusions as Eyler and Giles (1999). Astin and Sax (1998) looked at 42 national institutions and measured thirty-five student outcomes in five student cohorts from 1990 to 1994. Service participation was the independent variable in their body of work. Control variables included freshmen year pretests, service propensity, major, race, ethnicity, gender, and structural characteristics of the institution. All 35 student outcomes measured were favorably influenced by service participation. These included academic outcomes (GPA, retention, degree completion, amount of interaction with faculty, and increase in knowledge); civic responsibility (commitment to life goals of helping others and promoting racial understanding); and life skills (critical thinking, interpersonal skills, leadership skills, social self-confidence, knowledge of different races or cultures, and conflict resolution skills).

A 2014 study involving a community service-learning program at the University of Wisconsin found that both community partners and students benefitted from service-learning (McReynolds, 2014). Manegold et al. (2019) also reported that students benefitted academically and socially from the service-learning projects they administered. Tolan's (2007) study indicated that a service-learning experience positively correlates with the propensity toward participation in organizational citizenship behaviors when the service was engaged in by upper-level students and students with higher GPAs. Much research confirms the many ways in which organizations can prosper when their members participate in the prosocial organizational citizenship behaviors that are not necessarily part of their primary job descriptions (Podsakoff et al., 2000). Tolan's (2007) work should be of interest to employers who seek graduates who can add value to the business firm through their engagement in prosocial behaviors.

Interestingly, research involving service-learning has diminished after much excitement about this practice early in the new century. At that time, studies and reports such as those cited above were widely disseminated concerning service-learning applications and results. Since a well-orchestrated service-learning program requires commitment and resources, we suspect that the strain on resources in business programs in recent years has led to the stagnation of service-learning projects. Some of the issues with current administrative models regarding faculty that were discussed in earlier chapters might also deter faculty from participating in service-learning projects because of the commitment and labor that they require and the time that they will take from other research activities.

Dumas (2002) writes that service-learning in the management curriculum was avoided in the past; it may have seemed only appropriate for areas of study that were traditionally focused on the community. However, although additional efforts are needed, resuming these offerings would bring many benefits, especially by securing relationships between the college and the external business world.

More recently, in 2017, Hatcher et al. published a comprehensive volume on service-learning and its impact on various academic disciplines. Even in this carefully constructed report, the contributions to the book are all dated from the 20th and early 21st centuries, with the exception of one study from 2014. Hatcher et al. (2017) acknowledge that the practice of service-learning holds great promise for academic institutions, but inertia at academic institutions may be paralyzing, as we discussed in Chapter 4. They state:

When the degree and nature of the changes associated with service learning, and civic engagement more broadly, are assessed for their quality, breadth, and depth, interpretations vary. Saltmarsh, Giles, O'Meara, Sandmann, Ward and Bringle (2009) analyzed portfolios for the Carnegie Community Engagement Classification and found uneven evidence of institutional change; change had occurred in all classified institutions, but there was also evidence of resistance to change (e.g., in the arena of promotion and tenure), and there were consistent shortcomings (e.g., with respect to community campus reciprocity and community impact). Butlin's (2005) edited volume presented multiple perspectives that raised issues about the degree to which the assumptions, values, and operations of service-learning are incompatible with the ingrained culture of higher education, constraining the capacity of the pedagogy to generate transformational institutional change.

In order for service-learning programs to be appropriately developed and adopted, flexibility and modifications to the traditional operating systems of business schools are needed. We have elaborated on the problems that these inert models are currently presenting to academic institutions and remain hopeful that market forces will encourage schools of higher education to become more competent at preparing students for work in the new economy. Service-learning appears to be a very worthwhile tool towards this goal.

The "Fit" of Service-Learning Within Business Education

Role-playing, team projects, and case studies provide opportunities to simulate "real-world" practices and are essential tools for business educators. Although these are some of the most widely used methodologies to prepare business students for the workplace, "they can only approximate the 'culture' and complexity of non-academic situations" (Zlotkowski, 1996, p. 7) and often seem to offer less in the way of preparatory training than experiential experiences. Moreover, the content and process are weakened when separated (Lynton, 1993; Zlotkowski, 1996), which means that practitioners are best served when hands-on, practical experiences are merged with design activities and case studies so that students can master how to approach and deal with complex situations (Lynton, 1993). Berry and Chisholm (1999) report that Prof. Rex Taylor of the University of Glasgow, Scotland, has commented that "one of the defects of the modern world is the divorce between knowledge and experience.... The function of the university should be to marry knowledge with experience so that classroom-based learning is enriched by experiential learning" (p. 19).

Service-learning projects, in contrast, engage students with unsterilized situations in often-turbulent settings, and, if nurtured well, require creative and timely decision-making.

Service-learning opportunities help students to develop the additional competencies (breadth) that Porter and McKibbin (1988) discussed. According to the International Association for Management Education (formerly the American Association of Collegiate Schools of Business), all business graduates should embody the competencies and skills related to service-learning outcomes that research has uncovered. Benefits in the form of citizenship (Godfrey, 1999), leadership and conflict resolution (Thomas & Landau, 2002), teamwork, interaction, time management and networking (Tucker et al., 1998), cultural awareness and diversity (Vernon & Foster, 2002), and written and verbal communication (Crews & Stitt-Gohdes, 2012; Tucker et al., 1998) have all been reported in addition to the many benefits reported earlier in this chapter. Developing these skills—especially if they are transferable into cooperation through organizational citizenship behavior—should prove advantageous to American businesses. In addition, the value of service-learning opportunities has long been aligned with student engagement, global citizenship, and employability (Bennett et al., 2013; Salimbene, 2013); business programs should also be able to use such programs to gain a competitive advantage.

The International Assembly for Management Education (IACBE), an accrediting body of business programs, requires that business curricula provide an understanding of the ethical and social issues that form the context of business (Curriculum Content Guideline C.1.1.). Many of those who have conducted empirical research involving service-learning would argue that it is precisely the tool that could be applied to accomplish the goals of developing students towards these outcomes. For example, Gujarathi and McQuade (2002) wrote that corporations should not be solely to blame for being socially irresponsible if business schools do not contribute to the advancement of the community and do not convey the importance of corporate citizenship to their students, that is, those who will be running corporations in the future. Colleges that focus on developing students' ethical values will be able to provide ethically-minded and ethically-aware employees to organizations.

> Given that most organizations have a code of ethics actually in place or readily available, the critical problem in creating ethical organizations appears to be one of recruiting and retaining ethical personnel who will reinforce and instill ethical values in other organizational members. The best and most readily available source for such personnel are (sic) higher education institutions that have strong ethical cultures and skilled graduates. (Procario-Foley & Bean, 2002, p. 104)

Research findings display that community service enhances students' moral development (Boss, 1994; Boyd, 1980). Through service learning, students have opportunities to become ethically minded and ethically aware from their experiences and observations when dealing with external business entities.

In his publication, *The Good Society,* Robert Bellah (1991) discusses how major societal institutions, including higher education, can affect life choices and shape society. A takeaway is that through business education, business schools should also instill in individuals the desire to apply their knowledge and capabilities to make our global society a better place (Fisher, 1996). Through service-learning opportunities, which provide a bridge between academia and the workplace, colleges and universities are in a position to bring great value to students, businesses, and our global economy. Students get a glimpse of how businesses are run and can discern what is needed for businesses to be run in an ethical fashion. Further, students get to see real-world business problems that do not have easy solutions; they become responsible for critically thinking about ways in which they can impact outcomes. The service-learning partnering businesses also benefit from the perspectives and creativity of students.

A summary of the challenges facing management education that was developed by Dumas (2002) is presented in the chart below. This summary recognizes that management educators should be thinking about wide-reaching institutional changes as well as encouraging individual development. These recommendations have been shunned by many institutions in the years since they were proposed (see Table 5.1).

Service-learning may be viewed as a means by which to address these recommendations. DiPadova-Stocks (2005) notes, "Service-learning, properly designed and implemented, is grounded in the value of human dignity and the inherent worth of the individual. These values are fundamental to democracy and belong to all academic disciplines" (p. 352). Ideally, a service-learning program prepares students who are ready to participate as active citizens in a democratic society (Zlotkowski, 1996).

Service-Learning at Faith-Based Institutions

Faith-based colleges can better fulfill their missions and enrich the lives of their students by supporting service-learning collaborations with others in the community who are less fortunate. Connecting with the community in a meaningful way also serves to enhance a school's reputation. Moreover, faith-based schools can distinguish themselves by highlighting their heritage and mission through service-learning endeavors in ways that are visible and profound. Today there is a great need for ethical clarity by business leaders; it is an ideal time for educators at faith-based schools to provide this clarity in a way that can be transformative to students. Service-learning projects offer an excellent way for academic institutions to encourage ethical decision-making in "real-world" scenarios.

Table 5.1

Recommendations for Management Educators

- Develop integrated learning and eliminate silos of knowledge. Make connections between classroom learning, personal life, public issues, and involvement in the wider world.
- Help students actively construct knowledge and understand the importance of learning in complex contexts.
- Develop cooperative learning, using tools, addressing genuine problems in complex settings, involving knowledge applied to specific contexts.
- Reduce the gap between curricular content and the development of new competencies.
- Target the appropriate level of instruction to meet the needs of a wide range of knowledge levels.
- Integrate social and technical lessons to allow students to develop the higher-level cognitive skills they will need in practice.
- Enable students to become reflective practitioners by applying knowledge and principles used in the classroom to real-life problems and by using the experience to revise theories and develop knowledge in use.
- Develop in students interpersonal effectiveness (people skills), creativity, negotiation skills, aptitude for teamwork, ability to speak and write with clarity, responsibility and accountability, ethical values, time management, and decision-making and analytical ability.

Source: Dumas (2002, p. 253).

Service-Learning and Internships

Internships also provide experiential learning, or "learning by doing," but differ from service-learning projects in that the work involved with an internship may not necessarily align with course learning objectives. Unlike service-learning, internships are not necessarily in sync with classroom theory and reflection.

Moreover, internships, which have been the primary means to provide students with valuable work experiences, are often available to select students. Internships may also be more difficult to develop during an economic downturn, thus further limiting opportunities (WBUR, 2013). Asoka (2014) notes,

That internships are unpaid or poorly paid means that only those with means can even afford to take them, but that's where their "privilege" ends. Interns—predominantly young, inexperienced, temporary, and poorly protected—are the unrecognized workers at the very bottom of the professional food chain.

A distinguishing factor between internships and service-learning is not only the work setting—where meeting some social and community need is prioritized—but also the utilization of pedagogical strategies that promote reflection—both on the social dimensions of that need and on the learning process itself.

Conclusion

Although much time and effort may be needed to launch successful service-learning collaborations, many benefits accrue for colleges, students, organizations, and the community being served. Administrators at the highest levels of the college must be on board with the service-learning initiatives as adequate resources and respect for faculty who engage are necessary prerequisites for success.

There are challenges involved to administrators, faculty, students, and participating organizations in providing effective service-learning experiences that benefit all parties involved. The benefits, however, as highlighted above in this chapter, provide much evidence that these experiences can be invaluable. The chart developed by Tennessee State University (2023), and which is displayed in Appendix B, highlights benefits and challenges to students, faculty, and organizational partners. Traditional educational models to not present some of the challenges that we must overcome to make a service-learning experience a success; however, these traditional ways of delivering academic content are often far weaker at preparing students for work in the 21st century. Much research indicates that service-learning provides an excellent mechanism through which academic institutions can assist students in becoming ethical business leaders and citizens.

REFERENCES

Asoka, K. (2014, May 7). Internships aren't just cheap labor to abuse: They're workers—and they deserve pay. *The Guardian*. https://www.theguardian.com/commentisfree/2014/may/07/unpaid-internships-unfair-cheap-labor-abuse

Astin, A. W., & Sax, L. J. (1998). How undergraduates are affected by service participation. *Journal of College Student Development, 39*(3), 251–263.

Bellah, R. (1991). *The good society*, Knopf.

Bennett, W., & Wilezol, D. (2013). *Is college worth it?* Thomas Nelson Publishers.

Berry, H. A., & Chisholm, L. A. (1999). *Service-learning in higher education around the world: An initial look*. The International Partnership for Service Learning.

Boss, J. A. (1994). The effect of community service on the moral development of college ethics students. *Journal of Moral Development, 23*(2), 183–198.

Boyd, D. (1980). The condition of sophomoritis and its educational cure. *Journal of Moral Education*, *10*(1), 24–39.

Business Roundtable. (2019). *Business roundtable redefines the purpose of a corporation to promote 'an economy that serves all Americans*. Retrieved November 22, 2020, from https://www.businessroundtable.org/business-roundtable-redefines-the-purpose-of-a-corporation-to-promote-an-economy-that-serves-all-americans

Crews, T., & Stitt-Gohdes, W. (2012). Incorporating Facebook and Twitter in a service-learning project in a business communication course. *Business Communication Quarterly*, *75*(1), 76–79.

DiPadova, L. (2000). Service Learning Initiative. Academy of Management website, www.aom.pace.org

DiPadova-Stocks, L. N. (2005). Two major concerns about service-learning: What if we don't do it? And what if we do? *Academy of Management Learning & Education*, *4*(3), 345–353.

Dumas, C. (2002). Community-based service-learning: Does it have a role in management education? *International Journal of Value-Based Management*, *15*, 249–264.

Eyler, J. S., & Giles, D. E., Jr. (1999). *Where's the learning in service-learning?* Jossey-Bass.

Fisher, W. L. A. (2014). *The impact of service-learning on personal bias, cultural receptiveness, and civic dispositions*. State University of New York at Buffalo. ProQuest Dissertations Publishing.

Germain, M. (2019). *Integrating service-learning and consulting in distance education*. Emerald.

Godfrey, P. C. (1999). Service-learning, and management education: A call to action. *Journal of Management Inquiry*, *8*(4), 363–379.

Gujarathi, M. R., & McQuade, R. J. (2002, Jan/Feb.). Service-learning in business schools: A case study in an intermediate accounting course. *Journal of Education for Business*.

Hatcher, J., Bringle, R., & Hahn, T. (2017). *Research on student civic outcomes in service-learning*. Routledge.

IRS.gov. (2023). Retrieved on July 23, 2023, from https://www.irs.gov/individuals/irs-vita-grant-program

Jacoby, B. (1996). *Service-Learning in Today's Higher Education*. In B. Jacoby & Associates (Eds.), *Service-learning in higher education: Concepts and practices* (pp. 3–25). Jossey-Bass.

Lynton, E. (1993). *New concepts of professional expertise: liberal learning as part of career-oriented education*. New England Resource Center for Higher Education.

Madsen, S. (2004, July/August). Academic service learning in human resource education. *Journal of Education for Business*, *79*(6), 328–332.

Manegold, J., Schaffer, B., Arseneau, E., & Kauanui, S. (2019). Social innovation and poster presentations: Service-learning for business students in a team-based course. *Journal of Education for Business*, *95*(7), 469–475.

McReynolds, J. (2014). Service learning from the perspective of community partner organizations. *Journal of Undergraduate Research*, *XVII*, 1–10.

O'Neill, E. H. (1990). *The liberal tradition of civic education*. In J. C. Kendall & Associates (Eds.), *Combining service and learning: A resource book for community and public service* (Volume 1, pp. 190-200). National Society for Internships and Experiential Education.

Podsakoff, P. M., MacKenzie, S. B., Paine, J. B., & Bachrach, D. G. (2000). Organizational citizenship behaviors: A critical review of the theoretical and empirical literature and suggestions toward future research. *Journal of Management*, 26(3), 513–563.

Porter, L. W., & McKibbon, L. E. (1988). *Management education and development: Drift or thrust into the 21st century?* McGraw-Hill.

Procario-Foley E., & Bean, D. (2002). Institutions of higher education: Cornerstones in building ethical organizations. *Teaching Business Ethics*, 6, 101–111.

Salimbene, F. (2013). Service-Learning in business education: Stakeholders, project models, and international partnerships. *International Journal of Humanities and Social Science*, 3(10), 62–70.

Stanton, T. (1994). The critical incident journal. In A. A Watters & M. Ford (Eds.), *A guide for change: Resources for implementing community service writing*. McGraw-Hill.

Stoll, J. (2020, November 13). This degree is brought to you by Amazon. *The Wall Street Journal*. https://www.wsj.com/articles/this-college-degree-is-brought-to-you-by-amazon-11604941263

Thomas, K. M., & Landau, H. (2002). Organizational development students as engaged learners and reflective practitioners: The role of service-learning in teaching O.D. *Organization Development Journal*, 20(3), 88–100.

Tucker, M. L., McCarthy, A. M., Hoxmeier, J. C., & Lenk, M. M. (1998). Community service-learning increases communication skills across the business curriculum. *Business Communication Quarterly*, 88–99.

Tolan, M. (2007). *The relationship between student service-learning and participation in organizational citizenship behavior* [Dissertation from the University at Albany] State University of New York, published in ProQuest.

Thomas, K.M., & Landau, H. (2002). Organizational development students as engaged learners and reflective practitioners: The role of service-learning in teaching O.D. *Organization Development Journal*, 20(3), 88–100.

Tennessee State University. (2023). https://www.tnstate.edu/servicelearning/documents/Benefits%20and%20Challenges%20of%20Service%20Learning.pdf

Vernon, A., & Foster, L. (2002). Nonprofit agency perspectives of higher education service learning and volunteerism. *Journal of Nonprofit & Public Sector Marketing*, 10(2), 207–230.

WBUR On Point. (2013). *The internship economy. An interview on WBUR. June 11, 2013*. https://www.wbur.org/onpoint/2013/06/11/internship-economy

Weber, P., & Sleeper, B. (2002). Enriching student experiences: multi-disciplinary exercises in service-learning. *Teaching Business Ethics*, 7, 417–435.

Zlotkowski, E. (1996). *Opportunity for all: Linking service-learning and business education*. Journal of Business Ethics, 15(1), 5–20.

APPENDIX A

E-service Learning Projects by Degree Level

Degrees Courses	Associate Degree	Bachelor's Degree	Master's Degree	Doctoral Degree
Marketing	Branding solutions	Create email marketing campaign	Marketing strategy plan	Market research
Human Resources	• Development of employee policy • Employee satisfaction survey + results	• Hiring plan • Job descriptions • Employee motivation plan	• Employee handbook • Succession plan • Conflict and negotiation plan	• Company-wide compensation analysis • Analytics • Development of a formal and informal mentoring program
Law	Review of and advice on bylaws	Advice on 501(c)3 compliance	Advice on business partnerships	Advice on litigation
Accounting	Balance sheet and cash flow statement	Audit/Payroll	Financial predictions / forecast	Advanced financial analyses

(Appendices continued on next page)

APPENDIX B

Service-Learning Benefits and Challenges

Student Benefits	Student Challenges
• Working with unfamiliar populations reduces stereotypes and promotes tolerance • Promotes personal development, self efficacy, and leadership • Increases feeling of community connection and civic responsibility • Deepens understanding of subject matter and complexity of social issues	• Lack of time given the demands of school, work, and family • Fear of working with unfamiliar populations and issues • Lack of convenient transportation • Inability to relate service with their coursework and/or the work of the organization

Faculty Benefits	Faculty Challenges
• Expands role of educator from giver of knowledge to facilitator of learning • Inspires and innovates teaching methods • Broadens areas for research and publication related to current trends and issues • Promotes democratic citizenship and leadership and expands critical thinking and problem solving • Connects the community with curriculum and increases awareness of current societal issues as they relate to academic areas of interest	• Preparation work with the community partner and coordination of service activities requires time • Fear of unknown and letting go of control of the classroom when the impact of service learning is not easy to quantify in short term • Lack of institutional and departmental support given to faculty • Lack of time to adequately revise and restructure course in order to fully integrate service learning • Viewing service learning as soft, non-rigorous, non-academic learning or as an add-on, not an integral aspect of the course

Community Benefits	Community Challenges
• Opportunity to tap under-utilized volunteer base • Students often continue to volunteer beyond the end of the quarter • Students are enthusiastic and motivated to learn and bring with them new insights, perspectives, and knowledge • Extends community organization's ability to address unmet needs • Creates opportunities for community organizations to shape student learning	• Lack of time for preparation, training and supervision • Lack of benefit or even possible detriment resulting from short term volunteers • Difficulty recruiting students to work with organization due to location or type of work needed • Difficulty defining opportunities that meet student, faculty, and community goals

CHAPTER 6

ELEVATING THE COMMUNICATION SKILLS OF BUSINESS AND ACCOUNTING STUDENTS

ABSTRACT

In this chapter, we discuss the critiques that are leveled against business and accounting programs for their failure to develop the communication skills of their students. These programs often turn out graduates with the appropriate technical skills but with weak communication skills. Recognizing the rapidly changing skills and competencies required within the accounting profession, the American Institute of Certified Public Accountants (AICPA), and the National Association of State Boards of Accountancy (NASBA), designed a new accounting curriculum, referred to as the CPA Evolution, to revamp the accounting curriculum for college students in the United States.

The authors present, in this chapter, two specific exercises that have been effective in developing the communications competencies of accounting students.

Keywords: CPA evolution, communication skills, accounting curricula, business curricula

INTRODUCTION

A recurring theme in the critique of business education is the poor communication skills that graduates possess. As 2020 began, it was, perhaps, impossible to imagine how our world was about to change as COVID-19

A How-To Guide for Business School Practitioners, pp. 81–99

swept the globe. The implications on people's lives and the workplace would be long-lasting and would make us collectively reflect upon where we work and the way in which work gets done. Although this had been a developing concern, the pandemic also shed light on the importance of better communication skills among professionals and clients, especially among business and accounting professionals.

Doria et al. (2003) in discussing the inadequacies of many MBA programs, expresses that:

> Companies demand leaders who can powerfully articulate ideas, orally and in writing, to motivate and guide their people. But schools tend to train people to simply assert their ideas; they don't sensitize them to the critical value of being an excellent communicator.

Praxis.com, a company that matches college age students to full-time, paid internships reports that the College Learning Assessment Plus (CLA+), the standardized test taken by freshman and seniors at more than 200 colleges across the U.S. to measure how students' capabilities improved over the course of their studies, reveals in a 2013–2016 study that "business majors make considerably fewer gains in critical thinking, analytical reasoning, and writing and communication than science, engineering, and math students, as well as liberal arts majors (history, literature, philosophy, etc.). In addition, a DiscoverPraxis (n.d.) survey reports that 44% of employers felt that graduates' writing proficiency was inadequate, and 39% felt that graduates lack public speaking skills.

The results of this study formally present data that members of the CPA profession have officially recognized and acted upon. In Chapter 2, we discussed the growing concern among employers that graduates of business schools often do not have the communication skills that are critical to success in the workplace. Various reasons have been cited for this deficiency, including the growing dependency on technology, inadequate formative education and on the breakdown of communication among family members. Accounting firms have been especially vocal in their critique of the communication skills that accounting students possess when entering the workforce.

The Association of Chartered Certified Accountants (ACCA), a global professional organization for professional accountants, views accountancy as a vital cornerstone within society that exists to assist economies, organizations, and individuals to thrive by creating trusted financial and business management services. According to their research published in 2021:

> The paradox is this: in a world of work so innately technology led, the pandemic has exposed that work remains above all else a deeply human experience. This is particularly true of the accountancy profession as we look

towards the next decade. The work change we will see for accountants isn't just a transition to "hybrid work," a question of redesigning office spaces or finance teams with distributed footprints. It's much more fundamental. This is about a renewed sense of human connection and purpose, the opportunity for the profession to make a real difference that necessitates human as well as digital ingenuity. It's a story of skills transformation as jobs are re-imagined, work constructs are changed and careers are disrupted, and where technology advances either complement human endeavour, or where the current limitations of digital capabilities remain exposed. (ACCA, 2021, p. 7)

Accounting firms recognize that effective communication enhances the "human experience" and is, therefore, crucial for improved client relations and business growth. The challenge for many accounting firms has been finding accounting hires who, in addition to being educated in accounting and tax, possess the written and verbal communication skills needed to interact with colleagues and clients and to convey their specialized work to others. Based on the recent hiring data published by the Association of International Certified Professional Accountants (AICPA), accounting firms are hiring more and more non-accounting professionals as a means to overcome the limited communication and technological skills of accounting graduates who are entering the workplace.

Academic Education Versus Hiring Trends

In 2021, the AICPA reached out to nearly 25,000 public accounting firms and 1200 colleges and universities in the United States, generating a response rate of 3.3% from firms' business professionals and 6.4% from academia academics to provide hiring data within the accounting profession. As a result, in its 2021 biennial report, the AICPA reported on the number of new accounting and non-accounting hires by CPA firms as follows (see Figure 6.1; AICPA, 2021, p. 36).

Thus, according to this AICPA study, only 60% of new hires in 2020 by CPA firms in the U.S. are individuals with accounting backgrounds (60% tally as follows: 33% bachelor's in accounting, 19% master's in accounting, 2% master's in taxation, 1% MBA with a concentration in accounting, and 5% with a PhD in accounting). The AICPA states in this report, "New non-accounting graduates hired into accounting and finance functions have increased by 10 percentage points" (AICPA, 2021, p. 4). Further, in its 2019 report, the AICPA stated, "Across the last two *Trends* reports, we have experienced an approximate 30% decline in new accounting graduates. Non-accounting hires, as a percentage of all new graduate hires, are up 11 percentage points to 31% (AICPA, 2019, p. 5).

Figure 6.1

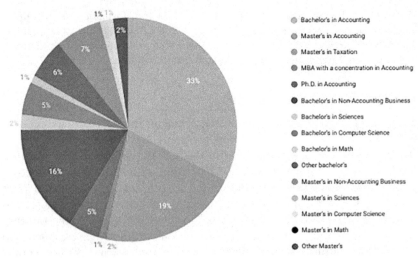

3.4 New graduate new hires hired into accounting/finance functions of U.S. CPA firms by degree — all degrees | 2020

This alarming trend of CPA firms hiring more and more non-accounting personnel motivated the AICPA to address why accounting graduates were no longer a match for the skills needed in the workplace. A glaring void was that accounting graduates lacked technical skills, such as competency in cybersecurity and data analytics, that were needed in the workplace. Also, due to the increasing volume of consulting services provided by accounting professionals, such as guidance on the 2020 Paycheck Protection Program (PPP) implemented during the pandemic, CPA firms need individuals with developed communication skills that accounting graduates had been lacking.

THE CPA EVOLUTION

Revamped Curriculum

To address the rapidly changing skills and competencies required within the accounting profession, the AICPA and the NASBA developed a new accounting curriculum for accounting students in higher education, known as the CPA Evolution, with input from CPA practitioners and academics. In their 2021 publication, the *CPA Evolution Model Curriculum*, the AICPA and NASBA unveiled their CPA Evolution curriculum requirements to revamp the higher education accounting curriculum in the U.S. by including a focus on (1) information systems and controls (IT), (2) tax compliance and planning, (3) business analysis and reporting, as well as the development of communication skills. Figure 6.2 highlights this new model.

Figure 6.2

Accordingly, the goal of the CPA Evolution is to better train accounting students with the technical skills needed in the workplace and the communication skills needed to better prepare students to serve and interact with clients.

Focus on Improved Communication Skills

Under Section 1, Module 8, Topic 6 of the 2021 CPA Evolution Model Curriculum publication, the AICPA and NASBA list seven learning objectives for accounting students regarding the communication skills needed for future accounting professionals:

Module 8: Financial Data Analytics

Topic 6: Communicating Accounting Data (Demonstrate ability to communicate accounting data analysis results.)

Learning Objectives

1. Demonstrate written communication skills (i.e., memos, emails, social media, reports, disclosures).

2. Demonstrate oral communication skills (i.e., mock interviews, role-playing, presentations).
3. Demonstrate visual communication skills (i.e., interpretation, mind maps, infographics, choosing appropriate visualizations, design best practices).
4. Demonstrate interpersonal communication skills (i.e., listening, situational awareness, emotional intelligence).
5. Explain key performance indicators (KPIs) on a dashboard.
6. List assumptions used in the analysis of data for financial decisions.
7. Identify targeted audience and scope of analysis (AICPA, 2019, p. 5).

Colleges and universities in the United States will be given a phase-in period to come into compliance with the mandates of the CPA Evolution. Each institution must decide how best to include and cover the required subject matter, which will involve reviewing and revamping existing courses or developing new ones. Although this will be an extensive undertaking, deliverables will be tangible—institutions must be able to demonstrate that they are including newly-required topics like cybersecurity, data analytics, and additional tax content in their curriculum. Perhaps the greater challenge will be demonstrating how effective communication skills are taught and instilled in students.

Business and accounting educators often claim that they train their students to be effective communicators. However, this involves helping students develop skills, which may involve a process that is more involved than the new curriculum tangibly exhibits; educators agonize over ways to help students become better communicators. Thus, assessing and demonstrating that students' communication skills have improved is a challenge.

Even for those who have "natural" writing and verbal communication abilities, communication skills need to be developed and honed through practice. Thus, to be better communicators, students need opportunities to improve these skills—they need practice to grow and feedback to fine-tune their skills.

We outline below two case studies (examples) of communications-based projects that are utilized in accounting courses and that have proven to be very helpful to the students in our courses.

Case Study #1 Feedback, Feedback, and More Feedback to Improve Communication Skills

Including written assignments, such as research projects, short-answer questions, and essay questions, as part of the course curriculum provides opportunities for students to practice their writing skills. With practice, students can become more comfortable with writing. However, to develop better communication skills, students need feedback.

To improve written communication skills, some instructors may request that students meet with their institution's writing resource centers to review grammar before the students' work can be graded. Other professors opt to provide their own feedback on grammar, as well as content. Written feedback—the assessment of grammar and content—provides a valuable learning component for students.

Feedback is also crucial for students to learn and develop better verbal communication skills. Accordingly, the challenge becomes how to provide this type of feedback within the curriculum of business and accounting course assignments. The following is an example of a project that covers course content while promoting teamwork and the development of verbal presentation skills:

Assignment Objectives

- To demonstrate proficient written and spoken communication skills in the analysis and presentation of audit research.
- To demonstrate effective teamwork as part of the audit process.

Assigned Auditing Research Project/Team Presentation

Objective
- To become acquainted with a publicly traded company's annual report and Form 10-K.
- To analyze and interpret the specific components of an audit report.
- To demonstrate effective teamwork as part of the audit process.
- To demonstrate proficient written and spoken communication skills in the analysis and presentation of audit research.

Students may work in groups of two and are responsible for an 8–10-page paper and a class presentation (15 minutes approximately) of their research.

Required
Obtain copies of the most recent Annual Report for the publicly traded company of your choice to address the following:

- What is the company's industry?
- What are its primary products?
- Who is the CEO?
- What raw materials (if any) does the company use?
- What are the company's sales, assets, and number of employees?
- Where are the location(s) and headquarters of your company?
- What other people/companies are closely associated with this company?
- How has your company been affected by recent economic events?
- What image does the annual report convey?
- What are the segments and functional contents of the report?
- What special accounting considerations are there, if any, for companies in this industry?
- Whose responsibility is it to prepare the financial statements?
- How does the 10-K differ from the Annual Report?
- Who are the auditors?
- What type of report was issued? (Please explain the components of the report.)
- What special auditing considerations, if any, seem problematic?
- Why are audit teams implemented as part of the audit process? Are they effective?
- If management faced tremendous pressure regarding the entity's financial performance, what opportunities might exist for them to engage in fraudulent financial reporting?
- Are sustainability matters addressed at all? Are assurance services applicable to this non-financial reporting?
- Does Sarbanes-Oxley impact the company or the preparation and audit of its financial statements?
- Do international auditing standards impact the company?

Students can be given a rubric to provide structure, so they know how to focus their efforts. For example, for this assignment, students used the following rubric as an assessment gauge:

Auditing Research Paper and Class Presentation Rubrics

Group Members: ---

CLASS PRESENTATION RUBRIC

	Beginning 1	Developing 2	Accomplished 3	Exemplary 4	Score
Class Presentation Content **Class Presentation Techniques**	Presentation is lacking in content and reflects poor preparation and collaboration. Students mumble, incorrectly pronounce terms and speak too quietly for the audience in the back of the class to hear. Students make no eye contact and only read from notes.	Presentation covers a few of the required questions and lacks collaborative organization. Students incorrectly pronounce terms. Audience members have difficulty hearing the presentation. Students occasionally use eye contact but still read mostly from notes.	Presentation covers many of the required questions but lacks collaborative organization. Voices are clear. Students pronounce most words correctly. Most audience members can hear the presentation. Students maintain eye contact most of the time but frequently return to notes.	Well-organized collaborative presentation that addresses all of the required questions. Students use a clear voice and correct, precise pronunciation of terms so that all audience members can hear the presentation. Students maintain eye contact with the audience, seldom returning to notes.	

| Collabora-tion & Com-pliance | The team lacks collaboration and has not met deadlines. Members of the group were inap-propriately dressed and did not man-age their time well. | Lacks group collaboration but has met deadlines for providing group information. Members were inap-propriately dressed but did manage their time well. | Shows evidence of group collaboration but has not met deadlines for providing group information. Members were dressed professionally but did not manage their time well. | Shows evidence of group col-laboration and has met deadlines for provid-ing group informa-tion. Mem-bers were dressed profession-ally and managed allotted time well. | |

RESEARCH PAPER RUBRIC

	Beginning 5	Developing 10	Accomplished 15	Exemplary 20	Score
Research Paper Con-tent (8-10 pages)	Poorly-written, poorly-researched paper.	Evidence of some research lacks responses to all required questions and is poorly writ-ten.	Evidence of research that incorporates required ques-tions but in-cludes many grammatical and spelling errors.	Well-writ-ten, well-researched paper that incorporates all required questions listed on the assignment page.	

(Rubrics provide structure and a more "objective" basis for assessment.)

Once the requirements are clear to students, they have a framework to follow and can proceed with their work. Thereafter, an effective way to provide feedback to students on their verbal presentations is to use "peer feedback" from classmates as follows:

Peer Assessments for Class Projects/Presentations

As students give class presentations alone or as part of a team, classmates are asked to provide constructive (and kind!) feedback. Their anonymously written comments can be collected after each presentation and given directly to the presenter(s) to keep and review. In order for classmates to know what to consider when assessing presenters, they can be given a checklist to complete, such as the following:

Student Presentation Checklist for Feedback to Class Presenter(s)

Presenters: _____

For each team presentation, please evaluate the following:

- **Delivery** (Presenters did not rush, showed enthusiasm, avoided *"likes, ums, you knows....."*
- **Eye Contact** (Presenters maintained effective eye contact and spoke to the whole class.)
- **Poise** (Presenters had good posture, faced the class, and seemed in control.)
- **Volume** (Presenters could easily be heard by all.)
- **Organization/Preparation** (Information was presented in a logical, interesting sequence that reflected preparation.)
- **Subject Knowledge** (Presenters demonstrated a full grasp and understanding of the material.)
- **Other Comments or Observations:**

Each item on the checklist can be reviewed in class so that students learn what is needed to make an effective presentation. Thus, before making presentations, students can review the checklist to know what presentation skills to work on and how their presentations will be assessed. Overall, presenters appreciate this structured feedback from their peers. As one student expressed:

I believe I benefitted greatly from the feedback I received regarding my presentation. Personally, I am not a very good public speaker; I never have been, so this was a tough one for me. It was honestly shocking to see that people said I did very well on the presentation. I was a nervous wreck up there, but no one seemed to notice. It goes back to that saying, "people perceive you half as nervous as you are," which clearly is a true statement. I feel that it was extremely helpful to have our peers, other than our professor, comment on our presentation because they can only critique so much, and our peers have different views and opinions on good and bad ways of presenting. It was extremely helpful to read the comments on things I need to work on so I can improve my public speaking skills for the future. This was a really good idea to have us write down our comments and observations because sometimes you do not know if you are doing anything wrong or right until someone points it out.

Further, in the next step of this feedback process, students are asked to comment on how they benefited (if at all) from the feedback they received from their classmates regarding their class presentations and teamwork. The following responses are sample comments received from student presenters:

- "I felt that the feedback I received was very beneficial. Understanding some of the little things that I do during a presentation, like looking at certain areas when speaking, will allow me to correct this in the future. Also getting feedback about our actual information—that the rest of the class thought it was good information—really helps. Part of the problem that I have when presenting is that I am not sure if the information I am giving should be in the presentation."
- "For the most part, the feedback from the class was positive. I mostly agreed with what they said we did wrong, especially regarding a clearer ending. I will definitely use what the class told me to improve my future presentations."
- "The information given as feedback was extremely helpful. My partner and I were very nervous before our presentation. We felt somewhat unprepared. The feedback calmed our nerves. My partner mentioned the feedback made her more comfortable with her public speaking skills."
- "Overall, I felt that the comments and observations made by the class were extremely helpful in assessing our overall presentation performance. I thought the evaluations were encouraging but critical in things that could have been improved. Like anything, some people are more critical than others. Therefore, these evaluations differed slightly in opinions. I really enjoyed this project as it not only gave us a better understanding of the extensity of detail that goes into the annual report presentation and audit reports as a whole, but it helped to practice and polish public speaking skills, which is not something that is addressed in every class. Public speaking skills are essential for individuals entering

the business world; however, many struggle with this skill set and lack this self-confidence."

- "Overall, my feedback was very positive. I am amazed that I seem comfortable presenting to the public when I feel like I cannot breathe. Many of the students mentioned good teamwork and knowledge of the information."

- "A few of the critiques I noticed were the use of our papers to help guide us. Normally in presentations, I use note cards and speak from memory. This presentation was different because of the extent of the information needed to be given. If I have another presentation in the future, I will try to memorize more facts. Another critique was that we could have put a picture slide of the information we spoke about, such as the financial numbers or audit report. We had tried to copy them into PowerPoint but could not do so. From watching another team present, I learned about the screen print they used to accomplish this. Now I know how to add more information in a picture matter for next time."

- "Feedback provided was useful. I was told my eye contact and volume were good. One helpful tip I received was my slides had too much information, so I should be better at condensing all the information I want to provide."

- "Most of the feedback from my peers was positive, but there were a few suggestions that I will certainly take into consideration. First was not to say 'um' as much, which I know I tend to do when I present. I can fix this by organizing my thoughts and taking my time while up in front of the class. The second was to split the talking up more evenly, which I also acknowledge. I tend to get a little anxious and keep talking while in front of the class. It was very rewarding, though, to receive such generally positive feedback."

The comments above indicate that students benefit by receiving feedback from their peers. In our experience, students reflect on the input they receive and can articulate they benefited. In addition, instructors can meet with presenters to ask them how they thought they did regarding points on the student presentation checklist. Instructors can also provide feedback regarding of the presentation as well as on presentation skills. The goal is for students to understand how to make an effective presentation with appropriate content coverage to understand their strengths and become aware of what is needed for improvement; thus, feedback, feedback, and more feedback help students further develop verbal communication skills!

Case Study #2—A "Professional Assignment" to Improve Communication Skills

Providing peer feedback for student presenters can work well as part of any assignment that includes a class presentation, whether in-person or virtual. It is also valuable for students to appreciate the importance of being able to communicate effectively as a key to success in their future careers. For instance, an assignment involving mentors allows students not only to grow their skills from feedback, but exposure to professionals in a professional environment is also a means for students to learn first-hand what is needed to thrive in the workplace; students become motivated to develop communication skills.

Although finding mentors for each student in a class may be daunting, there is often generous support from community professionals such as a local chapter of a professional organization like the New York State Society of Certified Public Accountants (NYSSCPA). In an accounting class, CPA mentors may be assigned to students based on student interest; forensic accounting mentors are often in great demand. In addition, structuring a mentorship as part of an academic curriculum is a dynamic growth opportunity for students that includes a service-learning component that may support the mission of a college or university.

The following is an example of a mentorship assignment that requires students to (1) reach out to mentors, (2) interview mentors, and (3) report and share mentorship experiences with the class.

Assignment Objective

To provide an opportunity for students to network with a mentor and further develop verbal and written communication skill—the "soft" skills—needed to excel in the workplace.

Requirements

1. **Email**—Students prepare email correspondences to mentors to request a virtual, phone, or in-person meeting. Email drafts will be discussed and reviewed in class.

Email drafts that students prepare for mentors become professional correspondences—no longer just an academic task. A good motivator is to offer a prize, like an NYSSCPA notepad, for the best introductory email to mentors; this exercise also promotes collaborative learning by having students review the writing of classmates. In addition, class presentations take on a professional quality when mentors are invited to attend and provide feedback. Students must also prepare an email correspondence to thank mentors and share feedback.

2. **Written Report**—Students prepare a report summarizing the mentor interview, including interview questions/responses and the "takeaway" or insights from the mentor assignment.
3. **Class Presentations**—Students prepare a PowerPoint presentation to share interview experiences and insights with the class; mentors are invited to attend.

Students can generate their own interview questions or choose from sample questions that can be provided:

- What are your responsibilities, and what do they entail?
- Which aspects of your work as a CPA do you find most challenging?
- As a CPA, what is your favorite type of work and why?
- How does busy (tax) season affect you?
- What is a typical day like for you at your firm?
- How do you handle your assigned workload?
- How do you balance your professional career and personal responsibilities?
- What was it that drew you to the accounting profession?
- From your experience, what would you say is the best strategy regarding the CPA exam?
- What advice would you give to a college student pursuing the CPA profession?
- How do you think Sustainability Accounting and Reporting (SAR) has affected or will affect financial reporting and the accounting profession?
- What is your view on the United States' convergence to IFRS?
- Based on your experience, what is the biggest challenge facing the accounting profession?
- Moving forward, how has COVID-19 affected firms and clients?
- What has been the impact of the CARE Act on businesses?
- How do you see the accounting profession changing as a result of COVID-19?

Mentorship Assignment: Student Feedback

Since a great deal of time and effort goes into arranging a mentorship assignment, it is important to get feedback from students to determine if students benefited or if changes should be implemented moving forward. It is rare to receive negative feedback from students regarding their work with mentors. The following is a sample of actual feedback from students who were asked to respond to the following:

Please indicate how you benefitted (if at all) from this mentor networking assignment.

- "This assignment gave me the knowledge and a look into life after college, which is something you don't usually learn in your classes."
- "I benefitted from this assignment in many ways. Not only did I get the chance to meet such a great person, but with the interview, I received a lot of great advice and strategies I can take with me for the rest of my accounting career."
- "I feel I connected strongly with my mentor, who gave me more clarity about the workforce. I was so grateful for all of the time given."
- "I did find this assignment to be valuable. It was nice to have the opportunity to talk with someone in my future profession."
- "Yes, it forced me to get out there and form connections with professionals in the accounting field."
- "Yes, I have a mentor for life!"
- "The mentor assignment is definitely valuable because you gain insight from professionals and make connections that you would not receive from the classroom alone."
- "Yes, it instilled a strong sense of professional responsibility." *No elaboration provided.*
- "Yes, meeting with my mentor was a great experience, and she had a great personality."
- "Yes, I did because I made so many connections and gained a forever mentor."

While students focused on this networking opportunity, they also were required to make a class presentation to share their mentorship experiences with the class. Thus, developing communication skills could be embedded into this assignment by having classmates provide feedback regarding class presentations. For this assignment, students were given a student presentation checklist that was similar to the checklist used in the auditing assignment above and provided the following reflections:

Please indicate how you benefitted (if at all) from the peer feedback you received from classmates regarding your mentorship presentation.

- "I thought the feedback from classmates was beneficial. One comment mentioned having a little too much information on my slides. I will be mindful and consider that in my next presentation."
- "Overall, feedback made me more confident about the upcoming presentation."
- "I had one comment saying at certain points, I rushed, which I agree with. This is something I feel I could improve."
- "I definitely benefitted from receiving feedback. Looking through my classmates' thoughts about my presentation was very reassuring. Not only did I see what improvements I needed to make, but with all the great compliments I received, my confidence in presenting has gone through the roof!"
- "I feel that I greatly benefitted from the peer feedback. I like hearing from my peers who were in a similar position as me. I appreciated the honest but kind feedback."
- "The feedback personally helped me a lot. I've always been unsure of my public speaking abilities and the feedback I received affirmed that I do get my points across and that I make good eye contact. I wish I had been given peer review feedback since Middle School when I started presenting for school-related assignments. Peer review should always be given for class assignments."
- "Having the feedback allowed me to see the positives and negatives of our presentation. It will help me greatly with my future presentations!"

To make the mentorship a genuine growth opportunity, students may be allowed to choose their meeting terms, i.e., via phone, virtual meeting, or in person. Some students may feel comfortable around professionals and the professional environment and may view the mentorship as an opportunity for a lifelong bond. Other students, who may not have been exposed to professional role models, may take more time to "warm-up" to a mentor. As they become familiar with the professional arena, students broaden their level of comfortability. They also grow by learning and recognizing the importance of conveying gratitude to their mentor for their service.

Most importantly, as students reach out to mentors through email, text, or phone, they develop and appreciate the need for practical "professional" communication skills. When students share their experiences with the class, they get practice in organizing and giving presentations. For instance, they can learn that PowerPoint slides can be used as an outline to keep a lecture flowing rather than being used as a list of items to read aloud. Students can be taught to face the class, make eye contact and prepare extensively so that each PowerPoint bullet triggers a talking point that keeps them on track.

Many assignments can be structured to include a feedback component from which students can improve their communication skills. This mentorship project also provides an excellent opportunity for students to get a taste of a professional environment and lessen their trepidation as they move closer to their future careers. In addition, while focusing on establishing professional connections, students can perhaps more confidently develop both written and verbal communication skills.

CONCLUSION

Evolving technologies and views defining the workplace have spurred change in the way business is conducted. As a result, there is a demand for different skillsets among business and accounting professionals, which includes more technical and better-developed communication skills. For the accounting profession, the AICPA and NASBA have taken the lead through the CPA Evolution to outline the new competencies and skillsets needed to make future accounting professionals a match for the demands in the modern workplace. The examples provided in this chapter provide some tools through which students in a technical major, such as accounting can become more astute in their communication abilities.

REFERENCES

Association of Chartered Certified Accountants (ACCA). (2021, September). *Professional accountants at the heart of sustainable organisations.* https://www.accaglobal.com/content/dam/ACCA_Global/professional-insights/pahso/PI-PATF-SUSTAINABLE-ORGANISATIONS.pdf

Association of International Certified Professional Accountants (AICPA). (2021). *2021 Trends Report.* https://www.thiswaytocpa.com/collectedmedia/files/trends-report-2021.pdf

Association of International Certified Professional Accountants (AICPA). (2019). *2019 Trends Report.* https://us.aicpa.org/content/dam/aicpa/interestareas/accountingeducation/newsandpublications/downloadabledocuments/2019-trends-report.pdf

AICPA/NASBA. (2021). *CPA Evolution Model Curriculum* (p. 5) https://thiswaytocpa.com/collectedmedia/files/cpa-evolution-model-curriculum-update.pdf

DiscoverPraxis.com. (n.d.). https://praxis.ets.org/on/demandware.static/-/Libra[Y.-Sites-ets-praxislibrary/default/pdfs/technical-manual.pdf

Doria, J., Rozanski, H., & Cohen, E. (2003, Fall). what business needs from business schools. *Leadership, 32*. https://www.strategy-business.com/article/03305

CHAPTER 7

THE NEED FOR BETTER QUANTITATIVE AND FINANCIAL LITERACY SKILLS

by Thomas Fitzmaurice

ABSTRACT

This chapter will look at the challenges facing college business programs, focusing on student deficiencies in both quantitative and financial literacy skills. After analyzing the potential reasons why high school graduates are not as prepared for the challenges in taking college level business courses, it will outline several potential solutions that will give students the opportunity to excel in higher level courses in a quantitative field of study like finance.

Keywords: Finance education, financial literacy, quantitative deficiencies

THE NEED FOR BETTER QUANTITATIVE AND FINANCIAL LITERACY SKILLS

The transition from high school to college provides both academic and social challenges for many students. Entering college with a solid foundation in mathematics is important for students pursuing a liberal arts major. For those pursing degrees in business, it is crucial. Often faced immediately with entry level courses in basic accounting and economics, graduating high school students lacking a solid mathematical foundation are at risk as they enter the door to college. In many cases, high schools are not

A How-To Guide for Business School Practitioners, pp. 101–115
Copyright © 2024 by Information Age Publishing
www.infoagepub.com

adequately preparing students with this foundation. This is an issue that seems to be increasing over time.

THE PROBLEM

High School Graduates Are Not Adequately Prepared in Math

Declining Math Scores on National and International Exams

The data over the past several years is backing up this alarming trend: U.S. students are less prepared according to their own standards. Twenty years ago, Steen (2001) concluded that most students graduate high school "with quantitative skills far below what they need to live well in today's society; businesses lament the lack of technical and quantitative skills of prospective employees; and virtually every college finds that many students need remedial mathematics." According to Steen, the results of data from the National Assessment of Educational Progress (NAEP) is not pretty, with "the average mathematics performance of seventeen-year-old students [is] in the lower half of the 'basic' range and well below the 'proficient' range" (pp. 286–336 & 336–367). The results have not improved since Steen acknowledged them. The most recent 2019 data shows 40% of 12th grade students below the NAEP basic level and only 24% at or above the NAEP proficient level (NAEP, 2019)

U.S. students are also falling behind their international counterparts in mathematics. The widely used Programme for International Student Assessment (PISA) exam data, produced by the Organisation for Economic Co-operation and Development (OECD) and measuring 15-year-olds' ability to meet real life challenges using mathematics, ranked the United States 32 out of 42 countries assessed (OECD, 2022). Recent trends in this data have not shown students in the U.S. achieving much progress in closing the gap. National Public Radio (NPR) went so far as to write an analysis of the poor results of U.S. students on a similar international math exam, summarizing with the title, "America's High School Graduates Look Like Other Countries' High School Dropouts" (Emanuel, 2016).

Why this is happening is a cause for much speculation. An article from *USA Today* outlined the issue that U.S. high schools teach math differently than other countries:

Classes here often focus on formulas and procedures rather than teaching students to think creatively about solving complex problems involving all sorts of mathematics, experts said. That makes it harder for students to compete globally, be it on an international exam or in colleges and careers that value sophisticated thinking and data science. (Richards, 2020)

Common Core State Standards

The issue that students in the United States are not learning math appropriately has been at the forefront of K–12 education for some time. We are only several years removed from the last major revision and upheaval in math (and other subjects) education: the Common Core State Standards (CCSS). These standards were touted by the U.S. Department of Education under President Barack Obama's $4.35 Billion Race to the Top initiative as a nationwide solution to these concerns. The CCSS was intended to find a common set of quality academic standards that all states could use, replacing the individual standards which varied greatly from state to state. Getting each state on board was a challenge, yet the potential benefits were promised by its leaders. According to a report by the National Governors Association (NGA, 2010), "The ultimate goal is for all American children to graduate high school ready for college, career pathways, and success in a global economy" (p. 1).

Initial data seemed to confirm the promise of better learning. As a result of the Race to the Top Initiative and the Common Core Standards, "The high school graduation rate hit an all-time high under President Obama, reaching 83.2 percent in 2014–15" (Sanchez & Turner, 2017). But while the country was graduating more high schools students than ever, there were concerns whether or not they were actually better prepared. Critics of the CCSS and its adoption process believed that, instead of being convinced that the standards were an improvement, states were coerced into adoption by the promise of federal dollars for their education programs. Reports followed that some states and districts may have developed strategies to artificially boost their graduation rates (Sanchez & Turner, 2017).

In many ways, the CCCS did not live up to its ideals. Instead of students gaining a deeper knowledge of core mathematical concepts, it caused confusion, resulting in no increase or in some cases a decreased understanding of these core concepts, as seen in the stagnant NAEP test data both prior to and after its implementation. Diane Ravitch, the former U.S. Assistant Secretary of Education, and a longtime proponent of national standards, concluded that the CCSS was not sufficient in providing standards that raise the level of education, saying, "We are a nation of guinea pigs, almost all trying an unknown new program at the same time (Ravitch, 2013). In recent years, some states have pivoted, and either adjusted the standards or in some cases abandoned them altogether. While proponents may consider this simply the trials and challenges of implementing a "revolutionary" change in teaching techniques, it does not help the generation of students who lost precious years as guinea pigs with a resulting foundational mathematical knowledge that is potentially keeping them behind the curve for years to come.

Grade Inflation

In looking to reconcile the data of increasing high school graduation rates at the same time as decreased international test scores, it invariably leads to another potential trend: grade inflation in high schools. A research report by ACT, the standardized test often used in conjunction with college admission applications, showed a steady increase in the mean High School Grade Point Average (HSGPA) with a corresponding decrease in the mean ACT score over the period of 2010–2021. The analysis suggested grade inflation was more of an issue at moderate and lower ACT Composite scores than it was for higher ACT Composite scores and that the number of students receiving B grades has decreased while the number of students receiving A grades has increased. The study made the conclusion that, "While the findings are neither surprising nor controversial, they do indicate a persistent, systemic problem" (Sanchez & Moore, 2022).

An analysis by *Forbes*, using data from the National Center of Education Statistics over the period of 2009–2019, showed a similar trend with the number of students taking more rigorous classes and the overall average GPA both increasing while test scores on mathematics fell. This is in conjunction with an increasing number of colleges nationwide eschewing the requirement of standardized tests like the SAT and ACT for college applications. This rapid trend, fueled by the effects of the recent pandemic in 2020, has led to an estimate that as many as three-quarters of America's colleges were test optional or test blind for the 2022 admissions year (Hess, 2022).

Standardized tests, whose proponents have long believed can level the playing field and correct for grade inflation, also need to be analyzed to see if they are artificially "moving the bar," as well. One potential example of this is the New York State Regents Exam in Algebra I, one of the longtime core high school math courses in the New York State high school curriculum. This statewide standardized exam, renamed Algebra I (Common Core) during the earlier part of the last decade, has since dropped the common core reference. The practice of converting a student's raw score (number questions answered correctly) and raw score percentage (raw score / total number of questions) on the exam into a scaled score using a published conversion chart has, however, has continued. Data from the

June 2022 Algebra I Regents Exam conversion chart (see appendix), shows the grade inflation, or curve (scaled score—raw score %) is more than 31 points for students receiving a scaled score of 65. In other words, in order to achieve a passing grade of "65" on the standardized exam, a student only needs to answer 31% of the questions correct. This grade adjustment has trended upward in recent years, as well. This fluid adjustment of the official final grades makes it more difficult to conclude whether or not an increasing number of students passing the exam each year is due to an increased mastery or simply a lowering of the standards.

High School Graduates Lack Financial Literacy Skills

Compounding the concerns of student preparedness in math, there is also an issue of business students, in particular, increasingly lacking in basic financial literacy knowledge. Today's students are required to be financially savvy. With increasing credit card and student loan debt, more diverse loan payment structures, and decisions to make regarding self-managed retirement accounts coming immediately after graduation, students and recent graduates are responsible for far more complex personal finances than those at their level a generation earlier. Unfortunately, there are a great number of college students lacking an even basic understanding of the responsibilities that many have already assumed. In a survey of incoming college students done by EverFi, a financial literacy-based software company, most respondents "struggled to answer basic financial literacy questions, and on average only answered two of six questions correctly" (Bidwell, 2018). This is not a problem for business students only. Preparing students for life after graduation should be a guiding principle for all in higher education, whether focusing on the classical education model of increasing personal and intellectual growth or focusing more on work-related skills and knowledge preparing for a career (Heimlich, 2011). A basic understanding of financial concepts now more than ever fits within both models.

Introductory finance courses, a requirement in nearly every business program, are often taken by students after their freshman year, when basic courses in accounting, economics, and management are completed. A deep knowledge of time value of money and risk/return concepts is often assumed and may only receive a basic review before moving on to more difficult quantitative mathematical concepts. In addition to an ever-increasing volume of financial terminology practically creating a language all its own, students without a solid foundation can quickly fall behind and feel as if they are "not good" at their chosen major.

Farrington (2021), in an article in Forbes highlighting the cost to students lacking financial literacy skills, stressed that, in addition to a required college level course on personal finance for all students in higher education, it is imperative that all levels of education lay the ground work for these necessary skills much earlier:

> Starting in elementary school, we need to start teaching personal finance concepts like budgeting, spending, and saving. As students progress into middle school and junior high, we can add in more advanced concepts like debt, interest, and how mortgages and car loans work. Finally, in high school, we need to be teaching our children about student loan debt and what they should expect. We should also cover practical concepts like how to check their credit score and what saving for retirement looks like.

Business School Graduates Lack Communication Skills

The previous chapter focused on the lack of communication skills seen among accounting students. While this chapter focuses mostly on finance students and the need for strengthening the quantitative and financial literacy knowledge of incoming freshman, we should note that a lack of communication skills is obviously not an issue confined to accounting alone. Hiring managers are most interested in seeing graduates improve their ability to communicate. Finance managers polled show that one of the skills most lacking in college graduates entering the workforce is communication (APQC, 2015).

This can be attributed, at least in part, to a similar lack of academic preparation in communication skills prior to and during a student's college years. However, other factors may be contributing, as well. The recent pandemic saw high school students adapt to an entirely new mode of education via Zoom or online class forums. This generation of students showed its ability to quickly adapt to the ever-changing modes of course delivery, often assisting their more technologically challenged teachers with their cyber skills. However, these pandemic related changes often came at the expense of the natural growth of communication and social skills at a critical time in their adolescent development.

For college finance students, an added detriment is the aforementioned unfamiliarity with basic financial literacy and terminology. In order to successfully communicate anything, it is essential to learn the language of those with whom you wish to communicate. Individuals lacking confidence in their language skills are often judged as overly quiet or non-opinionated when, in fact, they may have a lot of insightful and relevant things to say.

An article by the BBC surmises that confidence is the key for someone to quickly learn a new language. Having basic conversations with native speakers is a crucial first step in learning a language, as well as developing the courage to speak is necessary to make progress in a foreign language (Budden, 2015). Focusing on learning the language, or in this case, quantitative and financial literacy skills, and addressing deficiencies while providing practical opportunities to speak the language is a time-tested format for language learning programs.

POTENTIAL SOLUTIONS

While college business programs have no control over how high school courses are taught nor do they have the ability to address the issue of high school grade inflation, there are ways in which they can help to get their incoming students more quickly up to speed.

Co-Requisite Courses

Some college business programs give students the opportunity to take core business classes early in their college career, often as freshman. Introductory courses in accounting, finance, and marketing are often used to stimulate student interest in the various fields of business. Taking core courses early in the curriculum sequence allows students greater flexibility to choose a variety of high-level elective courses. This is important, as student choice and flexibility is a selling point for college admissions and business program recruitment.

However, the downside is that many students find themselves unprepared for the mathematical requirements necessary to properly pursue a course of study in business. Although a student's transcript may show completion of the necessary pre-requisite courses, an in-depth understanding of and an ability to apply this knowledge is greatly lacking. This causes issues across multiple courses. A student struggling with a math concept in economics will have the same problem in accounting. A struggling student becomes despondent when he or she concludes that they are simply not good at accounting or finance. However, the struggles they are experiencing in class may have nothing at all to do with accounting and finance and everything to do with a weakness in the application of basic mathematical skills.

In order to address this issue, students are often required to complete remedial coursework. This practice for incoming college students whose math scores are deemed below standard has been a standard practice for some time. Based on the results of a pre-matriculating competency exam, the college and business program determine up front the mathematical deficiencies of its incoming class. While this method counters the concerns of the curriculum offering core business classes too early in the program when students are not ready, this back loading of core courses in the curriculum can offer an entirely different dilemma. In recent years, based on the problems outlined at the beginning of the chapter, the need for remedial coursework often seems more like the rule than the exception. A student is delayed in his or her planned course of study until completing a full semester course (or courses) to address deficiencies, which may only require a refresher of previous material. Students taking one or more remedial courses often lose sight of its purpose, become indifferent to taking a course covering material already covered in high school, lose focus and interest in their chosen field of study, and may change majors prematurely. About one-third of students enrolled in bachelor's degree programs change majors within the first three years, led by mathematics and other STEM fields, which require strong quantitative skills (NCES, 2017).

There is an increasing belief that traditional remediation should be replaced by co-requisite remediation, which provides additional academic support for students without delaying entry into college-level classes. A recent study showed that students who took a college-level course with co-requisite supports earned more degrees, earned them faster, and, in the end, made more money than those students who completed remedial pre-requisite courses (Weissman, 2023). Co-requisite remediation, in this case, would involve a math or algebra course in conjunction with business courses as early as freshman year. Taking a math course at the same time as an introductory accounting or economics course not only provides efficiencies in which the math course can concurrently address challenges experienced in the business course, but it addresses the issue of alienating students from their desired course of study due to back loading business core courses to sophomore year or later. College business programs should work to carefully align the co-requisite courses so that the material is aligned in a timely manner. The instructors of the co-requisite courses should communicate directly, or the same instructor might teach both courses.

Early Core Finance Course

The problem of offering core classes too early or too late in the curriculum sequence is even more magnified for students interested in studying finance as a major or concentration. Finance is by its nature requires a higher level of mathematical expertise than the other specialty areas of business, and for this reason, the introductory level finance course often requires accounting and economics courses in addition to math courses like calculus and statistics as pre-requisites. This inherently puts finance programs at a disadvantage in engaging and enlisting students in the study of higher-level finance. A good compromise is the offering of a (very) introductory finance course as early as freshman year which combines basic math skills review and application as well as financial literacy skills with introductory course topics like time value of money, basic bond and stock pricing, and risk vs. return.

Assessing and Incorporating Math Review and Application

As with remediation, both with pre-requisite and co-requisite courses, the goal of the freshman introductory course is to give students the opportunity to strengthen their math foundation, allowing them greater opportunity to succeed in their major courses later on. This course would be taught as co-requisite for accounting, economic, and math courses, ensuring students have the opportunity to keep up while still maintaining or developing an interest in finance. As with the co-requisite programming discussed in the above section, the content of these courses needs to be tightly aligned so that the students can see the relationships between key mathematical and financial concepts.

While higher-level courses in finance may require college level statistics and calculus, a reliance on basic mathematical skills is essential at any level. Although all students have learned these basic skills at the primary and secondary level, they either do not retain this knowledge well after many years or do not have the in-depth understanding in order to practically apply the skills to finance. Adding and subtracting negative numbers, cross multiplication, and rate of change calculations are basic math concepts that students studied in their primary and secondary education classes. However, some still struggle when applying this knowledge years later to basic business and financial problems. Economics and marketing, for example, require a strong familiarity of the slope-intercept formula of a straight line in understanding the relationship between total cost, fixed cost, and variable cost. Students recall the basic equation to calculate a percentage change, yet are unable to quickly identify the need for its use in applying to problems analyzing financial data such as Gross Domestic Product (GDP) and the Consumer Price Index (CPI).

The financial industry has become more efficient due to the advancement and usage of technological tools. These have played a critical role in the growth of an industry, which has always placed an emphasis on the speed of calculating and analyzing data. The concurrent reliance on improving technology in high school (calculators, spreadsheets, etc.) comes with the downside of producing high school graduates with a greater ability to quickly calculate and retrieve data but also an increasing lack of ability to understand what and when to calculate.

A freshman year introductory finance course needs to ensure that students get in the habit of performing a quick "sanity check" after they calculate the answer to a financial problem—asking themselves whether or not the answer is reasonable and makes sense. For example, in calculating an estimate of the new price of a gallon of milk based on Consumer Price Index (CPI) data, a student will calculate a price increase even though the CPI Index declined over the same time period. They need to step back and look at the answer and the red flag will be apparent that something was done incorrectly. For a generation reliant upon the use of technology from an early age, students need to be reminded often of the old adage of "garbage in, garbage out" regarding the sometimes less than obvious equation of an incorrect input will result in an incorrect output.

The aforementioned CCCS math standards included standards based on the ability to estimate an answer based on given data. The CCSS Mathematical Standard developed to address this (MP1) states that in order to be mathematically proficient, students should check their answers to problems using a different method while continually asking themselves, "Does this make sense?" (CCSI, 2022). While these standards took a lot of criticism for allowing students to succeed without attaining a precise answer (close enough is good enough), the ability to quickly estimate in conjunction with requiring the calculation of a precise answer, is a skill that is invaluable in finance.

For example, students understand the basic time value of money equation, $FV = PV (1 + r)^n$, where FV is future value, PV is present value, r is the interest rate, and n is the number of compounding periods. Algebraically rearranging the equation to solve for the present value directly ($PV = FV / (1+r)^n$) is also quickly understood. The use of a financial calculator, a "black box" to which the value of the given inputs is simply entered quickly, producing an answer for the unknown variable, saves an enormous amount of time. Students however lose sight of the simple direct and indirect relationships that exist among the variables. Present value and interest rate have an indirect relationship. When a problem asks to solve for the present value and then recalculate when increasing the interest rate, students struggle with intuitively seeing that the present value must decrease with an increasing rate and other variables unchanged. This simple example highlights the challenge for a generation of students with strong technological skills seen in the ability to master the intricacies of a powerful financial calculator, yet an inability to estimate the result before "sharpening the pencil" to get the final answer.

A freshman level finance course should be constructed in order to ensure time for students to strengthen and combine both their estimation and calculation skills. As a rebuttal to the argument for the need for a full semester remediation math course, many students already have most of the tools needed, they just do not know how to use them. Reviewing these tools and, more importantly, understanding and communicating their utilization with others is essential, as the next section will elaborate.

Improve Communication Skills Through Immersion in Language of Finance

As described earlier, learning any new language usually starts with the study of basic vocabulary and syntax before infusing the opportunity to converse in the language. Foreign language classes quickly immerse students, often requiring them to speak exclusively in the new language when in the classroom. Learning the foreign language of finance should be approached in a similar way. Too often it is assumed that students know financial terms like risk, rate of return, volatility, and so on, particularly if the introductory course is taught in sophomore year or later. Students struggling with the language are often embarrassed to ask for clarification, as it is assumed that they are the only ones confused. Sufficient time in an introductory course should be allotted to define and discuss these terms both up front and as the course progresses continues with its quantitative requirements.

Gauging the class's financial literacy knowledge is the first step. The following is an example of a simple first day questionnaire.

1. Do you currently have a credit card?
2. If you have a credit card, do you pay the monthly minimum or something less than the full amount due each month?
3. Do you know approximately what the average interest rate (APR) is for credit card debt?
4. Do you have a student loan?
5. If you have a student loan, do you know the payment terms? List any information that you know (maturity of the loan; payback start date; interest rate).
6. Have you ever invested money in a brokerage account (stocks, bonds, cryptocurrency, etc.)?
7. What do you know about a NYS 529 account?
8. What do you know about an IRA?
9. What do you know about a 401k or 403b account?
10. Do you drive a car and have auto insurance?
11. Who is the owner of your auto insurance policy?

Reviewing the answers of the questionnaire/survey is a great starting point for beginning the financial language requirement. The answers usually show a wide variety of knowledge in the class. Students with a low level of knowledge are often relieved to know they are not the only ones in the dark. Others who have some knowledge benefit through discussions to learn how much they still need to learn. A freshman level introductory finance course which combines practical math review and basic financial topics augmented with a continuous development of financial language will better prepare students and instill confidence to tackle higher level courses.

Across all finance level courses, the immersion in the financial language must continue. Putting on the spot to discuss their views and opinions of current financial market conditions in conjunction with topics discussed in class works very well. The widely used lesson of allocating students a sum of money for investment in a mock trading portfolio is very popular in finance programs, creating a competitive environment among students to see who can make the most of an original investment. The practice of requiring students to regularly detail and communicate each investment decision as well as to formulate a market view, however, is the far more important learning outcome of the mock portfolio lesson. Students keep a daily or weekly log of all trading decisions, including taking profit and stop loss levels, in addition to being prepared to make impromptu oral updates to the class their regarding portfolio decisions. Much like the "market wrap" segments seen on financial news channels and the daily morning meetings held at Wall Street trading desks, a regular requirement to formulate opinions and views and communicate to others on a consistent basis works in a way that a separate, required public speaking course could not. Combining course content and language skills develops both confidence and, ultimately, the stronger communication skills that finance managers find are lacking in recent graduates.

REFERENCES

APQC. (2015). *The skills gap in entry level management accounting and finance: The problems, its consequences, and promising interventions.* https://docplayer.net/14250456-The-skills-gap-in-entry-level-management-accounting-and-finance-the-problem-its-consequences-and-promising-interventions.html

Bidwell, A. (2018, April 9). *Survey: Incoming college students struggle with basic financial literacy.* National Association of Student Financial Aid Administrators. Retrieved August 8, 2021, from https://www.nasfaa.org/news-item/14855/Survey_Incoming_College_Students_Struggle_With_Basic_Financial_Literacy

Budden, R. (2015). *The secret of learning a language—quickly.* BBC. Retrieved September 23, 2022, from https://www.bbc.com/worklife/article/20150302-secrets-to-learning-a-language

Emanuel, G. (March 10, 2016) *America's high school graduates look like other countries' high school dropouts.* NprEd. Retrieved August 8, 2022, from https://www.npr.org/sections/ed/2016/03/10/469831485/americas-high-school-graduates-look-like-other-countries-high-school-dropouts

Farrington, R. (2014, July 16). *The financial literacy gap costs college graduates thousands.* Forbes.com. Retrieved September 20, 2021, from https://www.forbes.com/sites/robertfarrington/2014/07/16/the-financial-literacy-gap-costs-college-graduates-thousands/?sh=5efc97e54fb2

Heimlich, R. (2011, June 2). *Purpose of college education.* Pew Research Center. Retrieved July 30, 2021, from https://www.pewresearch.org/fact-tank/2011/06/02/purpose-of-college-education/

Hess, F. (2022, March 30). *High school grade inflation is a problem: Getting rid of the SAT would make it worse.* Forbes. Retrieved July 22, 2022, from https://www.forbes.com/sites/frederickhess/2022/03/30/high-school-grade-inflation-is-a-problem-getting-rid-of-the-sat-would-make-it-worse/?sh=7d61674dae7a

NAEP. (2019). *The Nation's Report Card. NAEP Report Card: Mathematics.* Retrieved October 15, 2022, from https://www.nationsreportcard.gov/mathematics/nation/achievement/?grade=12

NCES. (2017). *Beginning college students who change their major within 3 years of enrollment. U.S. Department of Education.* Data Point. NCES 2018-434. Retrieved October 16, 2022, from https://nces.ed.gov/pubs2018/2018434.pdf

NGA. (2010). (ED583243. files.eric.ed.gov)

OECD. (2022). *Mathematics performance* (PISA) (indicator). Retrieved August 28, 2022, from https://doi.org/10.1787/04711c74-en

Ravitch, D. (2013, February 26). *Why I cannot support the common core* [Web blog]. http://dianeravitch.net/2013/02/26/why-i-cannot-support-the-common-core-standards/

Richards, E. (2020, February). *Math scores stink in America. Other countries teach it differently—and see higher achievement.* USA Today. Retrieved September 1, 2022, from https://www.usatoday.com/story/news/education/2020/02/28/math-scores-high-school-lessons-freakonomics-pisa-algebra-geometry/4835742002/

Sanchez, E., & Moore, R. (2022, May) *Grade inflation continues to grow in the past decade.* ACT Research Report. Retrieved Aug 13, 2022, from https://www.act.org/content/dam/act/secured/documents/pdfs/Grade-Inflation-Continues-to-Grow-in-the-Past-Decade-Final-Accessible.pdf

Sanchez, C., & Turner, C. (2017, January 13). *Obama's impact on American schools.* NPR. Retrieved September 5, 2022, from https://www.npr.org/sections/ed/2017/01/13/500421608/obamas-impact-on-americas-schools

Steen, L. A. (Ed.). (2001). *mathematics and democracy: the case for quantitative literacy.* National Council on Education and the Disciplines.

Weissman, S. (2023). *Study: Better outcomes for students in corequisite courses.* Inside Higher Ed. Retrieved January 11, 2023, https://www.insidehighered.com/quicktakes/2023/01/11/study-better-outcomes-students-corequisite-courses

APPENDIX

The State Education Department/The University of the State of New York

Regents Examination in Algebra I—June 2022

* Data retrieved from the Chart for Converting Total Test Raw Scores to Final Exam Scores (Scale Scores)

https://www.nysedregents.org/algebraone/622/algone62022-cc.pdf

Raw Score*	Scale Score*	Raw %	Curve	Raw Score*	Scale Score*	Raw %	Curve	Raw Score*	Scale Score*	Raw %	Curve
86	100	100	0	57	81	66	15	28	66	33	33
85	99	99	0	56	81	65	16	27	65	31	34
84	97	98	(1)	55	80	64	16	26	64	30	34
83	96	97	(1)	54	80	63	17	25	63	29	34
82	95	95	(0)	53	80	62	18	24	61	28	33
81	94	94	0	52	80	60	20	23	60	27	33
80	93	93	0	51	79	59	20	22	59	26	33
79	92	92	0	50	79	58	21	21	57	24	33
78	91	91	0	49	79	57	22	20	56	23	33
77	90	90	0	48	78	56	22	19	55	22	33
76	89	88	1	47	78	55	23	18	52	21	31
75	88	87	1	46	78	53	25	17	50	20	30
74	88	86	2	45	77	52	25	16	48	19	29
73	87	85	2	44	77	51	26	15	46	17	29
72	86	84	2	43	77	50	27	14	44	16	28
71	86	83	3	42	76	49	27	13	42	15	27
70	86	81	5	41	76	48	28	12	40	14	26
69	85	80	5	40	75	47	28	11	37	13	24
68	84	79	5	39	75	45	30	10	34	12	22
67	84	78	6	38	74	44	30	9	32	10	22
66	84	77	7	37	74	43	31	8	29	9	20
65	83	76	7	36	73	42	31	7	26	8	18
64	83	74	9	35	72	41	31	6	23	7	16
63	83	73	10	34	72	40	32	5	19	6	13
62	82	72	10	33	71	38	33	4	16	5	11
61	82	71	11	32	70	37	33	3	12	3	9

60	82	70	12	31	69	36	33	2	8	2	6
59	81	69	12	30	68	35	33	1	4	1	3
58	81	67	14	29	67	34	33	0	0	0	0

CHAPTER 8

BUSINESS ETHICS AND WHY IT MATTERS FOR SCHOOLS OF BUSINESS

by Charles Zola

ABSTRACT

This chapter provides a historical overview of the study of ethics along with an examination of the nature of ethics and how it relates to business. The author discusses the need for business ethics in the business curriculum and how it should be addressed.

INTRODUCTION

A brief or cursory review of daily business news will readily reveal some type of illegal or morally questionable activity occurring somewhere in the business world. Ethical breaches may be as small as a local grocery store intentionally selling products past their sell-by date in the hope of making some profit off of unsuspecting customers or as large as using insider information to an unfair advantage in purchasing stock. The occurrences of unethical conduct may seem so commonplace that one can easily understand the popularity of the disparaging observation that business ethics is an oxymoron. It seems that many professionals and businesses care little for doing the right thing despite a societal expectation that they should. Given this, one can't help but wonder: business ethics, why bother?

A How-To Guide for Business School Practitioners, pp. 117–131
Copyright © 2024 by Information Age Publishing
www.infoagepub.com

In this chapter, I will argue that ethics does indeed matter in the business world. To do so, I will first examine the nature of ethics and how it relates to business. Second, I will consider business ethics as part of a business curriculum. Last, I will propose why this study is essential even if ethical lapses continue to occur. In my analysis, I use the term "business" in a very broad way. I intend a common sense meaning that describes the exchange of goods and services between or among agents for money or financial gain. This exchange entails many other activities ranging from study and professional expertise, design and research, supply chain and production, marketing and advertising, pricing and selling that in themselves rely upon a multitude of workers and organizations. These transactions ultimately depend upon consumers and occur at the local, regional, national, and global levels of human society with various degrees of government involvement.

Ethics

To begin, I will situate this topic within a broader philosophical framework. Each discipline and investigation—from astronomy to zoology—is defined by a goal or purpose. For example, the study of biology is defined as the study of life, and this objective provides the means for establishing the methodology of research and limits the purview by which the investigation will proceed. The study of ethics is no different.

If asked to explain what the discipline of ethics is about, most would reply that is has to do with investigating the nature of what is right and wrong, just and unjust, or moral and immoral. One finds a family resemblance among the terms used to describe this field of study. Put simply, ethics is concerned with studying and evaluating human action in terms of its goodness or badness. However, this is only a half-truth as the study pre-supposes a more fundamental matter. One should ask "why" such ideas are of interest in the first place. Why study the concepts of good and evil or justice and injustice?

This same question can be posed for any other field of study: why bother studying life, literature, mathematics or language? For some disciplines the study is pursued as an end in itself because humans have a natural curiosity about the world in which they live. For some, it is just satisfying to know things. On the other hand, the pursuit of knowledge serves a useful purpose as it permits one "to do" things with the knowledge or information gained. This is apparent in the tech fields where study and investigation can build a better computer system or make communication easier. Whereas the physicist is able to unlock the structure of the atom, technology can use the information to create a nuclear weapon. This distinction between knowing for its own sake and knowing for the sake of usefulness is an important one for clarifying the nature of business ethics.

If ethics involves the study of the nature of right and wrong or good and evil, is it merely for the ideal of knowing because it is just good to know or because it has some practical outcome. We should ask ourselves what are the practical implications of the study of ethics. Why bother studying ethics? What can I do with it? A clue lies in considering the etymology of the term.

Our English word "ethics" is derived from the Greek word ***ethos*** which means "character" or "custom." The Greek word ***ethos*** translates into Latin as ***mores*** from which we derive the English terms "morals" and "morality," two other words often associated with ethics. For the Greeks, the study of ethics was concerned with a study of the customs or characteristic actions of everyday human life. That is, how is it that a human being lives, not merely as a living organism among thousands of other living beings, but as a living being that determines its own end or purpose through the power of reason and by acting upon its choices. As rational, the human being is does not merely react to its environment and stimuli but directs itself to be understood and chosen outcomes in the present or remote future.

Unlike other animals who merely interact with their environment in customary or characteristic ways—dogs do dog things, trees do tree things—the human animal is able to think about and direct its actions to a number of desired ends, everything from sailing a ship, waging a war, to boiling water. None of these actions are determined to happen or occur by chance, they are the result of rational deliberation and chosen actions. But such actions are not ultimate, they are directed to a higher or superior end. Aristotle points out that without a final goal or purpose, human activity would be pointless and lack fulfillment (ca. 350 B.C.E.). This goal he had defined as happiness or living life well. For Aristotle, the activities of human life were not merely about living life per se, but about living *a certain kind of life*. The human being ultimately desires happiness or to live life well, and all our deliberations and choices orient ourselves in this direction.

It is precisely because human reason is defective and the human will can be weak that attention needs to be paid to those customs or actions that human beings engage in because they result in either achieving the goal of happiness or missing the mark. Therefore, ethics as the study and evaluation of human action is not pursued merely for its own sake, but because it has a practical outcome. In fact, it is this outcome which is the only one that ultimately matters.

Today, ethics is divided into two main branches: theoretical ethics and practical ethics. The former is concerned with understanding the nature of moral good and evil actions as well as the normative actions or obligations that are rooted in these concepts. The latter focuses on the application of these ethical norms to the resolution of ethical dilemmas that arise in a broad range of human activities like health care, law, and business.

While commonplace today, courses in business ethics and appreciation for the moral dimensions of business have not always been a standard in academe. There has been a gradual evolution in appreciating the way that ethics has exerted a subtle influence in shaping and regulating the myriad dimensions of contemporary business practice. In a "History of Business Ethics," De George (2015). distinguishes three meanings of ethics as it relates to the practice of business: ethics in business, business ethics as an academic field, and business ethics as a movement. This classification is incredibly helpful for providing a framework by which to approach the topic and facilitates an understanding of why business ethics matters for schools of business.

Ethics and Business

Let us consider ethics as a theory and how it relates to business. Obviously, our everyday lives are influenced and regulated by generally agreed upon moral principles such as respect, civility, justice, and honesty. The formal articulation of these moral principles has been the consequence of much human reflection, study, and discussion spanning thousands of years. These moral principles express values that are inherently constitutive for relationships among family members, between friends, and society as whole. They have had a long evolution of development and are often appealed to in considering the way business is regulated. As such basic ethical principles are found in everyday life and in business as well.

De George (2015) argues that the two greatest forces to have exerted influence in this regard is the Judeo-Christian moral tradition and Western philosophy.[1] For example, the Jewish moral tradition as articulated in the Decalogue or Ten Commandments condemns lying and coveting your neighbor's property. In addition, there are moral norms concerning observing a respect for the land and fidelity to promises. Christianity obviously inherited and preserved key moral principles of Judaism and expanded upon them. Jesus advocated the sharing of material goods not only with friends but enemies as well, compared the generosity of God the Father to the generosity of a land owner toward laborers in the field, and the necessity of developing one's gifted talents in order to return a profit to one's employer.

The Western philosophical tradition has also contributed to the vocabulary of ethical norms applicable in the practice of business. For example, the concept of justice as a regulation of one's appetite for material goods and pleasure is an important moral principle in Plato's concept of virtue (ca. 360 B.C.E.). The idea was further developed by Aristotle in his treatment of moral virtue as a moderation between the excess and deficiency in human action (ca. 350 B.C.E.). For both these philosophers, regulation of such desire is an essential means to the end of finding happiness and essential in the regulation of a well-ordered society. It would be very difficult to live a happy life if one had to live with those who commit injustice.

Later, Christianity's dual commandments of love of God and love of neighbor would inspire philosophers like Augustine and Thomas Aquinas to further develop the concept of justice as a moral virtue and compliment it with the supernatural and highest Christian virtue, charity. Moreover, Aquinas examines the vice of greed and the proper attitude toward material possessions (ca. 1265–1274). Having inherited, preserved and expanded upon the virtue ethics tradition of ancient Greek philosophy, Christianity cultivated a moral sensitivity to the concerns and needs of the poor and marginalized that—although not always perfectly practiced—recognized and promoted a respect for persons, property, and the use and distribution of resources.

Post-Reformation theology provided the intellectual grounds for the development of the Protestant work ethic by Max Weber (ca. 1904–1905) and Enlightenment philosophers contributed to the development of the concept of human rights, the responsibilities and limits of government, as well as the importance of self-determination. In the mid-18th century, Adam Smith's *An Inquiry into the Nature and Causes of the Wealth of the Nations* (1776) was preceded by a work in moral philosophy that is often forgotten, *The Theory of Moral Sentiments* (1759). In it, he articulated how the human being was an interplay between two contrasting but complimentary forces: egoism and sympathy. These human characteristics provided an explanation for how goods and services are naturally transferred and are the basis of his theory of the Invisible Hand, which naturally moves the market along in the ebb and flow of supply and demand.

Historical developments in business beginning in the 19th and continuing through the 21st century have generated responses from the disciplines of theology and philosophy that have helped to raise societal consciousness of moral values pertinent to business. This is especially evident in considering Catholic social teaching and political philosophy.

The consequences of mass industrialization in the nineteenth century gave rise to Pope Leo X's 1891 encyclical *Rerum Novarum*. Rooted in Natural Law and Catholic moral teaching, the document focused on the exploitation of workers and their moral right to unionize balanced against the legitimate right to private property and the pursuit of a just profit by owners or capitalists. This balanced defense of both private property and the rights of workers was sustained and subsequently reaffirmed 100 years later in Pope John Paul II's encyclical *Centesimus Annus* (1991). As an intellectual who came of age in post-World War II Poland where communism was imposed upon it by the USSR, John Paul II was adept in tackling the moral issues at stake in the competing ideologies of capitalism and socialism. More recently, Pope Francis's 2015 encyclical, *Laudato si'*, draws particular attention to the interplay of how care for the environment is intimately linked to the issues of poverty and economic injustice.

Political philosophy of the 19th century was interested in addressing the rapid changes brought about by growing industrialization and mass consumption. Marx and Engels (1848) helped to usher in great political and social changes due to their theories concerning the value of labor and the alienation of workers in the face of massive and ever-increasing industrialization. Later, Marx would argue forcefully against laissez-faire capitalism in his *Das Kapital* (1867).

This short survey has highlighted how both the Western moral tradition and the Judeo-Christian religious tradition have helped to shape contemporary moral values as they relate to business. Among some of the most prized moral norms are respect for persons and property, justice, virtue, character, and responsibility. These values permeate the cultural and societal expectations that most people have concerning how business operates and are foundational for legal codes.

The second way that business ethics is understood is as an academic field. In his analysis, De George (2015) points out that the post-World War II years had ushered in much social change in America; it was a time that American business grew due to the post-war economic boom, the growing chemical industry, globalization, and the exploitation of natural resources. American society became more critical about the growing role of business and started to hold business accountable for their newfound economic power. The response of business was to create programs that addressed these social issues, and the concept of corporate social responsibility was born. Schools of business started to follow this lead and courses developed centered on this theme, but they approached the issue primarily from the point of view of managers and the laws. Little attention was paid to the application of ethical norms to these social issues, but things were about to change.

Traditionally, academic philosophers and business faculty had little to say to each other. The ethicists did not view business as a worthy area of study, and for their part, business faculty did not think that the disciplines of philosophy or ethics could contribute anything to the discipline of business. However, things started to change with the publication of John Rawls's work, *A Theory of Justice* (1971) which was an important work on political philosophy, bringing together ethical theory, economics, and distributive justice. A conversation soon began between the boardroom and classroom. Academicians began to see how ethics could contribute to the practice business, encouraging business to think and act with greater social responsibility, and businesses recognized that ethicists might have something to say that could help in their articulation of social responsibility. The dialogue among academic ethicists, philosophers and business people resulted in an "intersection of ethical theory with empirical studies and the analysis of cases and issues" (DeGeorge, 2015).

The first conference on business ethics was held at the University of Kansas in 1974 and by 1980, the Society for Business Ethics was started hosting its first meeting in conjunction with the American Philosophical Association. Many other groups began to spring up like The International Association for Business and Society, The European Business Ethics Network, and the International Society for Business, Economics, and Ethics. The first issue of the *Journal of Business Ethics* appeared in February 1982; the first issue of the *Business Ethics Quarterly* in January 1991; and the first issue of *Business Ethics: A European Review* in January 1992.

The importance of ethics in the business curriculum was firmly established by the mid-1980s with more than 500 courses taught across the country to 40,000 students and more than 20 textbooks and 10 case study textbooks. Further strengthening the academic focus on business ethics, many colleges and universities opened centers and institutes dedicated to the topic of business ethics or incorporated the topic in its programming.

The last way that business ethics can be understood is as a movement. De George defines it as "the development of structures internal to the corporation that help it and its employees act ethically, as opposed to structures that provide incentives to act unethically" (DeGeorge, 2015). Perhaps one of the most important catalysts that prompted businesses to examine how they address ethics within the workplace has been a series of federal laws that seek to protect the rights of workers; among these are: the Equal Pay Act of 1963, the Civil Rights Act of 1964, the Age Discrimination in Employment Act of 1967 and the Americans with Disabilities Act of 1990. These federal laws as well as others at the state and local levels, required businesses to level the playing field in all areas of business from the application process, job placement, promotion, and even discipline and discharge.

Beyond conformity to legal sanctions, most businesses have developed clearly stated responsibilities for employees within the organization and have started to employ ombudsmen or chief ethics officer to make sure that the businesses hold themselves morally accountable for their policies. One of the chief ways that businesses have become morally cognizant is through the articulation of their values in mission statements and even incorporating ethics trainings as part of their business culture. More recent developments in businesses have been a renewed sense of corporate social responsibility in terms of environmental sustainability and addressing issues related to diversity, equity and inclusion.

This overview of the relevance of ethics for the practice of business has revealed several points. First, the way businesses operate or conduct themselves has evolved not only in terms of the products or services they sell but also in terms of how business understands itself in relation to issue of ethics and morality. Second, as business has evolved, society has increasingly held businesses accountable for their actions both internally and externally. While profit may be the endgame of a business, society has an expectation that business will play that game according to a set of moral principles and with a sense of responsibility for the wider community within which it operates at both the local and global levels. Perhaps, it may be argued that both these trajectories are not isolated but rather two sides of the same coin, each informing the other. Given these dual expectations, it is not unrealistic to expect that business ethics should be considered an essential component of the business curriculum.

Business Ethics and the Curriculum

The topic of teaching ethics or moral education is millennia old. A deep dive into that history is beyond the scope of this chapter. However, both the Judeo-Christian and Western philosophical traditions that I have just referred to advocate instruction for the young in regard to morality and right living: "Train children in the right way, and when old, they will not go astray" (Proverbs 22:6); "Take to your heart all the words with which I am warning you today, which you shall command your sons to observe carefully, even all the words of this law" (Deuteronomy 32:46), and "Fathers, do not provoke your children to anger, but bring them up in the discipline and instruction of the Lord" (Ephesians 6:4).

The same attitude is found in the moral philosophies of Plato and Aristotle. In the *Republic*, Plato argues that moral education is crucial for a well-governed state, and the education and upbringing of children is of crucial importance (ca. 360 B.C.E.) Later, his student, Aristotle, would work out a much more detailed analysis of the matter concerning virtue in the *Nicomachean Ethics*. Aristotle was realistic in his observation that young people are bad students of ethics and politics because they are swayed too easily swayed by their emotions and have little experience of the world. Yet, he still insisted that children be trained in the right habits from their youth (ca. 350 B.C.E.).

The importance of moral education in terms of the current business curriculum is explicitly affirmed and its inclusion is expected. All three of the top accrediting agencies for schools of business require that they demonstrate a commitment to moral education in their curriculum. In 2004, the Ethics in Education Task Force of the Association to Advance Collegiate

Schools of Business (Business, Ethics Education in Business Schools, 2004) issued a report that called upon schools of business "to renew and revitalize their commitment to the centrality of ethical responsibility at both the individual and corporate levels in preparing business leaders for the twenty-first century" (Business, Ethics Education in Business Schools, 2004, p. 9) In its 2020 accrediting standards, the AACSB (Business, 2020 Guiding Principles and Standards for Business Accreditation, 2020; updated July 2022) lists ethics and integrity as the first guiding principle and expectation for accredited schools: "The school encourages and supports ethical behavior and integrity by students, faculty, administrators, and staff in all its activities" (Business, 2020 Guiding Principles and Standards for Business Accreditation, 2020; updated July 2022, p. 17). In addition, Standard Four which deals with curriculum content states that curriculum content be influenced by the "mission, values, and culture of the school" (Business, 2020 Guiding Principles and Standards for Business Accreditation, 2020; updated July 2022, p. 41) and "curricular elements within formal coursework that promotes a positive societal impact" (Business, 2020 Guiding Principles and Standards for Business Accreditation, 2020; updated July 2022, p. 43)

The Accreditation Council for Business Schools and Programs (Programs, Standards and Criteria for Demonstrating Excellence in Business Degree Programs, 2021) outlines curriculum requirements in Standard Six (Programs, Standards and Criteria for Demonstrating Excellence in Business Degree Programs, 2021, pp. 40–49). All four levels of programs (associate, baccalaureate, master's, and doctoral) specifically include ethics as an integral part of business education. The requirement is included within the accreditation standards of a larger section entitled, the business environment, which also includes topics on business and law, the global dimensions of business, economics, and business communications.

Last, the International Accreditation Council for Business Education (IACBE) has a separate line-item criterion in its *New Program Self-Study Manual: Accreditation Principles and Evaluation Criteria* (Education I. A., New Program Self-Study Manual: Accreditation Principles and Evaluation Criteria, 2019). In its iteration of Characteristics of Excellence in Business Education (Education I. A., New Program Self-Study Manual: Accreditation Principles and Evaluation Criteria, 2019, pp. 3–4), the council makes several observations related to ethics and the curriculum. The curriculum should cultivate students who are not only professionally prepared but are also "well-educated, ethical and competent business professionals" (Education I. A., New Program Self-Study Manual: Accreditation Principles and Evaluation Criteria, 2019, p. 4) and the faculty "integrate ethical viewpoints and principles in their teaching activities" (Education I. A.,

New Program Self-Study Manual: Accreditation Principles and Evaluation Criteria, 2019, p. 4).

While it is reassuring that the three main accrediting bodies for schools of business recognize the value of incorporating ethics into the curriculum, it also raises a quandary. If moral education or business ethics courses are integral to a business school curriculum, why do ethical breaches in a business environment continue to happen? Moral education in terms of business is not a new phenomenon. As we observed, it has been around for at least four decades. We may, therefore, legitimately ask if all the textbooks and courses in business ethics have done any good. What is it that a course in business ethics hopes to achieve? What are its learning outcomes? While it is easy for accreditors to require ethics in the curriculum, it is much more difficult to define what this should look like. And even if one can agree upon the point of a course in business ethics, what are the means to that end?

As can be imagined, much has been written in response to these fundamental questions over the course of the several decades since ethics and business have become an explicit and focused area of concern. The vast amount of literature on the issue attests that there is still debate about what the goals of business ethics education are and there is still no definite and universal answer about the optimal way to teach business ethics or how to achieve those goals once they have been agreed upon. It is curious to note that even in 1991—after nearly 30 years of discussion to elevate the topic in the boardroom and the classroom—Robert Meyers lamented the fact that many individuals in the business community held the view of a "dual standard of ethics" that distinguished between one's personal ethics and those that one practiced in the workplace (Meyers, 1991, p. A9). Fast forward to the present: the situation has not greatly improved. While the accreditors require ethics to be an integral part of the business curriculum, they are not overly proscriptive about how the end is to be achieved. This presents a challenging but exciting opportunity to continue to engage in dialogue and research on the matter.

The question of how business ethics should be taught hinges to a large degree upon what the objectives of a business ethics course are, as the ends will determine the means. Daniel Callahan's "Goals in the Teaching of Ethics" (Callahan, 1980) distinguishes five goals relevant to all ethics courses, regardless of level or context. They offer insight and guidance for consideration for a business curriculum. Briefly described, they are:

1. Stimulating the moral imagination. Students need to be "provoked" or made aware of moral dimensions of life that is occasioned by our daily interactions with one another. We form relationships and act in ways that impact these relationships at

both the personal and community levels. Actions have consequences for which we are held responsible, and our choices can make one happy or miserable or cause suffering. The power of imagination helps to raise awareness of morality, especially through the media of movies, plays, and novels. Emotional responses to this stimulation can convey "moral messages" and students need to be made aware that there is "the possible difference between what they *feel* to be right or good, and what *is* right or good. Callahan calls this the "premoral" stage (Callahan, 1980, pp. 64–65).

2. Recognizing ethical issues. The emotional responses just spoken of present an opportunity to move from the realm of feeling to thinking. There must be a "conscious, rational attempt to sort out those elements in emotional responses" (Callahan, 1980, p. 65). What is the proper response to a feeling of injustice or the violation of autonomy? The rules and moral principles offered in the discipline of ethics provide a framework for organizing and evaluating these emotional responses. In doing so, students begin to explain or reason about those emotional responses.

3. Eliciting a sense of moral obligation. An appreciation for the ethical dimensions of a moral question may lead to a sterile outcome. That is, students may be able to determine and appreciate the moral theories that are relevant to a particular situation but have no desire to do anything about it. To put is simply, one may recognize the good that is to be pursued and the evil to be avoided, but there is no desire to do so. As a moral agent, we are not merely thinking beings, but beings that "will to act on the basis of our judgment" (Callahan, 1980, p. 66). An ethics course should prompt or "stimulate" students to want to do what has been deemed morally correct action. Of course, the caution to be exercised here is not to cross the line from "education to indoctrination" but this can be done by emphasizing the importance of personal moral responsibility for one's action or inaction.

4. Developing analytic skills. In addition to recognizing how moral principles and ethical theories relate to lived experience, students need to be encouraged to critique and analyze these principles and values. Callahan calls this the development of "logical skills" wherein the analysis of morals requires "coherence and consistency" in how these principles are applied and in evaluating the outcomes of moral choices (Callahan, 1980, p. 67). In short, students need to be reflective and evaluative

about the ethical principles themselves and in how they are applied to the dilemma at hand.

5. Tolerating—and reducing—and disagreement and ambiguity. A natural outcome of this analysis will be the recognition that several competing theories or answers can be found to one moral question. And these disagreements do not simply stand without more examination. According to Callahan, "What often separates ethics from other kinds of intellectual analysis is the necessity of constantly examining the most basic premises of the entire enterprise" (Callahan, 1980, p. 67). While disagreements exist in all disciplines, ethics, when confronting the resolution of a dilemma, it is not simply resolving the issue, but calling again into question why the issue is important in the first place. Divergent and contrasting moral viewpoints are an obvious feature of doing ethics, but as a discipline, ethics is continually trying to clarify issues and moral principles to reduce ambiguity and minimize such disagreements. Attention must be directed toward finding common ground or shared values. As moral agents, we are ultimately responsible for our own moral choices, but we live in a network of relationships with others or in a moral community. Our individual moral lives are influenced by the actions of others, and ethics should help us learn to tolerate moral differences without necessarily abandoning our own moral principles.

These foregoing objectives are important as they recognize both the rational and emotional capacities of the moral agent in navigating moral waters. Doing ethics is not merely applying previously established moral norms or principles to the resolution of an ethical dilemma, as if one can simply select the correct formula and plug it into the equation or calculate an answer like solving a math problem. Callahan's analysis recommends that an ethics course must sensitize students to the reason why ethics is important in the first place and how ethical decision making relates to a greater framework of interpersonal relationships. If this is so, then I propose that in the business context, the study of ethics can help students realize that the primary aim of ethical decision making is to help them find self-fulfillment or happiness both personally and professionally, and this pursuit has ramifications for the flourishing of business writ large.

Business Ethics, Why It Matters

The Western ethical tradition has emphasized that ethics is not merely about achieving happiness but doing so with the right intention and as an expression of one's character. The nexus between making morally good choices and happiness is not limited to one's personal life but translates into the business world as well. If students in business school are to benefit from courses in business ethics and if these courses are to meet the learning objectives of accrediting agencies, then courses in business ethics should develop this connection. As Robert Solomon (1994) states, "Ethical thinking is ultimately no more than considering oneself and one's company as citizens of the business community and of the larger society, with some concern for the well-being of others and—the mirror image of this—respect for oneself and one's character" (p. 65). He challenges the prevailing view that business ethics is a matter of simply calculating how ethical theory is applied to resolving a dilemma arising in business. Rather, he proposes, "It [business ethics] is the foundation of business. Business life thrives on competition, but it survives on the basis of its ethics" (p. 38). In short, the success of a business and those who pursue a career in business arises—in part—because of focusing attention on moral decision making and the moral character of those involved in the practice, not despite it.

This is an incredibly important observation as it emphasizes that ethics is about what we do on an everyday basis. Its starting point is human activity. As observed earlier, we live in a network of relationships that are imbued with moral value and whose sustenance and health depend upon some basic moral principles, like fairness, honesty, and common courtesy. In turn, these relationships keep society and business running, even if they are not always exercised everywhere. No one gets it right all the time, and everyone has moral failings. If the study of ethics—business or otherwise—is to be good for anything, it should propose to engage us in the question of finding happiness through our everyday choices and discerning how these choices contribute to or deviate from the goal of happiness. To do so is not indoctrination but rather an aid in helping to identify how we can fulfill the most basic and universal human desire. The study of ethics invites us to examine our own values and moral codes in light of more than two thousand years of collective wisdom and challenge us to defend them when alternative viewpoints are proposed.

If the foregoing is correct, we should expect that what is ethical behavior outside the workplace should carry over into the workplace. As Peter Drucker (1981) puts it, "There is only one ethics, one set of rules of morality, one code—that of individual behavior, in which the same rules apply to everyone alike" (p. 3). If family unity and friendships depend upon honesty, loyalty, and good will, we should expect the same in the business world.

This view may help us distinguish between ethical blunders in themselves and culpability for those missteps. Ethical lapses may arise due to a lack of knowledge or a defect of the will. In such cases, we evaluate the culpability of a moral agent in terms of these circumstances. Did they have enough information? Was too much pressure placed upon them? Did they fully understand what was happening and what was at stake? Depending upon that analysis, responsibility for that ethical mistake may be adjusted accordingly, and there is an expectation that the moral agent ideally commits to making better choices in the future. This stands in sharp contrast to unethical behavior that is intentionally pursued due to greed, anger, or lack of concern for justice. The second type of moral failure is more difficult to deal with, as it reveals something of the moral agent's very character. We may very well ask them, "What kind of a person does something like that?"

Seen in this light, the moral infractions we witness in business are to be expected and will—given the frailty and limitations of human nature—continue to happen, just as they occur in countless ways outside the business environment. While accrediting bodies for schools of business can require ethics courses in the curriculum, in themselves, these courses will not guarantee to prevent unethical behavior in the future. However, that does not negate their importance.

As a discipline, ethics invites us to engage in a study of fundamental and universal human importance and which has a universal appeal that is rooted in moral character. I propose that the answer to the question why bother about business ethics is rather simple. Ethics matters because happiness and living a good life matter in the workplace or outside of it. As centers where students learn the discipline and craft of business, it is important that schools of business do not neglect this crucial aspect of professional development. Not only is ethics integral in the practice of business, but its study contributes greatly to the individual happiness and satisfaction that students hope to enjoy in their future careers. Rather than seeing business ethics as a discipline that is "tacked on" to the rest of the curriculum, business ethics is an integral part of business education and one that schools of business must take seriously.

REFERENCES

Aquinas, T. (n.d.). *Summa theologiae*. Benzinger Brothers.

Aristotle. (n.d.). *Nichomachean ethics*. Penguin Classics.

Business, A. t. (2004). *Ethics education in business schools*. AACSB. https://www.aacsb.edu/-/media/publications/research-reports/ethics-education.pdf?la=en

Business, A. t. (2020; updated July 2022). *2020 Guiding Principles and Standards for Business Accreditation*. Association to Advance Collegiate Schools of Business. https://www.aacsb.edu/-/media/documents/accreditation/2020-aacsb-business-accreditation-standards-jul-1-2022.pdf?rev=b40ee40b26a14d4185c504d00bade58f&hash=9B649E9B8413DFD660C6C2AFAAD10429

Callahan, D. (Ed.). (1980). Goals in the teaching of ethics. In *Ethics teaching in higher education* (pp. 61–80). The Hastings Center.

DeGeorge, R. (n.d.). *A history of business ethics.* Markkula Center for Applied Ethics. https://www.scu.edu/ethics/focus-areas/business-ethics/resources/a-history-of-business-ethics/#eight

Drucker, P. (1981). What is business ethics? *The McKinsey Quarterly,* 2–15.

Education, I. A. (2018). *New program self-study manuel: Accreditation principles and evaluation criteria.*

Education, I. A. (2019). *New program self-study manual: Accreditation principles and evaluation criteria.* https://iacbe.org/accreditation/

Education, I. A. (n.d.). *New program self-study manuel accreditation standards and evaluation criteria.*

Marx, K. (1867). *Das Kapital.* Penguin Classics.

Marx, K., & Engels, F. (1848). *The communist manifesto.* Penguin Classics.

Meyers, R. J. (1991, March 3). The indivisibility of ethics. *New York Times,* p. A9.

Plato. (n.d.). *The Republic.* Penguin Classics.

Programs, A. C. (2021). *Standards and criteria for demonstrating excellence in business degree programs.* Accreditation Council for Business Schools and Programs.

Programs, A. C. (2021). *Standards and criteria for demonstrating excellence in business degree programs.* Accreditation Council for Business Schools and Programs.

Rawls, J. (1971). *A theory of justice.* Belknap Press.

Smith, A. (1759). *The theory of moral sentiments.* Penguin Classics,

Smith, A. (1776). *An inquiry into the nature and causes of the wealth of nations.* Penguin Classics.

Solomon, R. C. (1994). *The new world of business: Ethics and free enterprise in the global 1990s.* Rowman and Littlefield.

Weber, M. (1904-05). *The Protestant ethics and the spirit of capitalism.* Penguin Twentieth Century Classics.

X, P. L. (1891). *Rerum Novarum.*

ENDNOTE

1. In this analysis of how theoretical ethics has influenced business practice, I have followed De George's (2015) analysis but have added some examples not found in his text and omitted others.

CHAPTER 9

SURVIVAL AND GROWTH

ABSTRACT

When we returned to our college campuses after the global pandemic, it quickly became apparent to us that the academic world that we had worked in for many years had been permanently transformed. Although the shifting tides had begun years earlier, the realities of market forces that had been ignored by so many colleges were finally recognized. Student enrollment did not rebound to pre-pandemic levels, but government support initially helped with financial operations, providing another distraction away from the issues that were pressing down. The private colleges that we worked at and that employed many of our colleagues are now struggling in ways that must be addressed if they are to survive. Traditional consumers of college education—including the students, their families, and employers—have begun to pursue more economical alternatives and novel career preparation models instead, and these alternative routes further threaten institutions of higher education. It is not too late to institute business models that focus on differentiation of services and cost efficiencies; two things that have been previously lacking in many institutions of higher learning.

Keywords: strategic management, business models, differentiation, efficiencies

A CHANGED LANDSCAPE

As we discussed in the early chapters of this book, the securing of college-ready students has become a highly competitive activity, especially now that many students are substituting the traditional college experience with other types of enrichment activities. These other activities include—but are not limited to—attending community colleges, receiving vocational

A How-To Guide for Business School Practitioners, pp. 133–136

training, taking part in technology boot camps, obtaining employer-provided training, and joining the military. Numerous studies are indicating that the college degree cannot bring the returns that it once did, and that this reality is impacting families who are strained by the 2022 recession and the residual effects of the pandemic. Many are also taking a pause from traditional college education in response to the debacle of the student loan crisis. In addition, widely publicized studies—some of which we have cited in this book—have indicated that students receiving a baccalaureate degree are often ill-prepared for the workplace.

In 2021, Preston Cooper, from the Foundation for Research on Equal Opportunity, performed a comprehensive review of the Return on Investment from college programs and found that:

> For students who graduate on time, the median bachelor's degree has a net ROI of $306,000. But some degrees are worth millions of dollars, while others have no net financial value at all.

> After accounting for the risk of dropping out, ROI for the median bachelor's degree drops to $129,000. Over a quarter of programs have negative ROI.

> Four in five engineering programs have ROI above $500,000, but the same is true for just 1% of psychology programs.

> Elite schools such as Caltech and Penn dominate the list of highest ROI programs. But attending an elite school is not a golden ticket; some Ivy League degrees have negative ROI.

These figures further validate our position that strategic business models need to be both developed and adhered to by institutions of higher learning if these institutions are to experience sustained profitability and growth. Some of the proposed strategies that we provide in the first eight chapters of this book can serve to help strengthen colleges administratively and may provide specific guidance to business school professionals that can assist in improving their programs.

Strategy Enacted

Chapter 2 is entitled "Strategy is Lacking" and details the ways in which college administrators have often displayed an aloof disposition toward business models and to the profit motive. In our experience, colleges and universities continually draft college-wide strategic plans that are—in theory—supposed to trickle down to academic and operating departments. These academic and operating departmental units then draft and pursue their own related plans. All too often, these plans contain abstract constructs that are difficult to measure and to operationalize. Assessment is a topic that is continuously discussed in academic life and educators seek to employ a variety of assessment tools. As we have discussed, academic programs are continually assessed so that they may receive a stamp of approval from accrediting bodies. The holistic health of these institutions of higher learning is, however, often largely ignored, except through admissions statistics.

A business strategy course often provides capstone experience for students majoring in business management. From what we witness at many colleges, this course is designed to combine and synthesize material from all of the major business disciplines so that students can prepare for the interrelated, synergistic demands of the organizational world. Strategy is formally defined as "an integrated and coordinated set of commitments and actions designed to exploit core competencies and gain a competitive advantage" (Hitt et al., 2020). This definition clearly establishes that the goals of a strategy must be pursued by all parties and all departments within an organization. As we discussed earlier, many college administrators, especially those at small and medium-sized institutions, do not view their roles as having a strategic focus. All too often, responses to problems are reactive instead of proactive and the path of least resistance is taken with regard to operational difficulties. Support is provided to programs that are faddish or that are poorly performing, instead of those that will reap success into the future—and that will teach those skills that employers are demanding. Strategic management would require that all employees at a college or university work in lockstep towards the pursuit of a vision that is clearly articulated and continually highlighted. All too often, we see strategic plans discussed at the highest levels of the academic institution that fail to impact employees and students in individual departments.

Michael Porter (1998) is a preeminent Harvard professor and author on strategy who has elevated thinking about the topic of strategy for over 40 years. In his book, *Competitive Advantage* (1998), he discusses business-level strategies that can create differences between the firm's position and those of its competitors. He suggests that to achieve a sustainable competitive advantage, a firm (in this case, a college or university) can either perform its activities differently than competitors or can perform different activities than them. These types of business-level strategies are necessary today, in the competitive higher-education environment, if these institutions are going to succeed. This can be done, as Porter has continually emphasized, by integrating the activities the organization performs in ways that create superior value for their customers or consumers. This can come about in many ways, such as through incorporating interdisciplinary, innovative programming, ensuring rigor in coursework, uniting with other entities through strategic alliances and providing novel career preparation and placement programs. This type of differentiation can also be realized through a focus on the service providers, who are the faculty who are at the front lines with the consumers. This can be done, potentially, through the hiring and promotion of more faculty practitioners who have excelled in the contemporary workplace. Greater attention should be paid to faculty performance evaluations, and they should become related to the achievement of each faculty member and its relationship to the well-being of the entire institution. In addition, greater efficiency in the delivery of services should be a priority and should result in cost reductions for consumers. This option has rarely been considered in academia, based on historical data detailing cost, and associated tuition increases.

We believe that those institutions that can provide employers with students who possess the desired skill sets—communications, quantitative reasoning abilities, ethical decision-making abilities, and the ability to thoughtfully interact with others—will be able to compete effectively and achieve a sustainable competitive advantage, often without the added expenses of over-the-top amenities and excessive peripheral student services. Although these add-ons and student support services are desired by students to some degree, they cannot be the primary reason for a college's existence.

Colleges that are open to fulfilling their mission toward the broader good instead of simply serving insiders—administrators, faculty, and service staff—will be those who stand out among their competitors and who survive the transformation that is currently underway.

REFERENCES

Cooper, P. (2001). *Is college worth it? A comprehensive return on investment analysis.* FREOPP (The Foundation for Research on Equal Opportunity). https://freopp.org/is-college-worth-it-a-comprehensive-return-on-investment-analysis-1b2ad17f84c8

Hitt, M., Ireland, R. D., & Hoskisson, R. (2020). *Strategic management—Competitiveness and globalization.* Cengage.

Porter, M. (1998). *Competitive advantage.* Free Press.

ABOUT THE AUTHORS

Moira Tolan, PhD

Dr. Tolan began her early career in business management and professional sales in New York's financial district. In 1992, she began teaching
at Mount Saint Mary College in Newburgh, NY and rose to Professor of
Business. For many years, Dr. Tolan also served as the Coordinator of Business Graduate Programs at the school. Since 2013, she has been an elected
member of the Board of Directors at the Northeast Business and Economics Association (NBEA) for which she served as Conference Chair/Vice
President and editor of their proceedings journal.

Dr. Tolan's research and publications focus on how to improve management education. She has co-authored a 2022 book entitled *Sustainability
Accounting and Reporting: The Evolution of Management Accountability* with
Tracey Niemotko and was a contributing author to *Adolescence in the 21st
Century: Constants and Challenges* in 2013. In addition, Dr. Tolan has written
many articles which discuss ways in which management education can improve so that students can be better prepared for the modern workplace.

Dr. Tolan earned her PhD at the State University of New York at Albany
and her BBA and MBA at Iona College in New Rochelle, NY.

Tracey Niemotko, JD, CPA, CFE

Tracey J. Niemotko, a Fordham University and Fordham University School
of Law graduate, is a licensed attorney-at-law, certified public accountant,

and certified fraud examiner. Prof. Niemotko has enjoyed teaching accounting for many years and has been a member of the New York State Society of Certified Public Accountants since 1991.

According to *Accounting Today*, which included her among the Top 100 Most Influential People in 2022, "While she's an academic, there's nothing of the ivory tower about Niemotko, from her roles on the AICPA's Governing Council and with the New York State Society of CPAs, and her focus on the future of accounting education, to her recently published book on sustainability accounting and her engagement with shaping climate disclosure standards." Although she may not be perceived as being part of the "ivory tower," Prof. Niemotko has worked in higher education for nearly four decades and is able to share her observations regarding academia in this publication.

Prof. Niemotko currently serves as the Chair of the Department of Accounting and the Director of the Master of Science in Public Accountancy Program at Marist College in Poughkeepsie, New York.